Pocket Pickler

Essential recipes
for pickles, chutneys,
relishes and more

Pocket
Pickler

Essential recipes for pickles, chutneys, relishes and more

Alex Elliott-Howery
CORNERSMITH

murdoch books
Sydney | London

CONTENTS

Introduction

There's so much to love about pickling.
Delicious, low waste, from-scratch cooking
that is easy, good for your budget, helps you
understand the seasons and avoid packaging
and additives, and makes a great gift. On top
of all that, it's really good fun.

I've been pickling for over 15 years. It all
started when my partner, Jimmy, who loves
growing food in small spaces, filled our tiny
backyard with zucchinis. We were overloaded.
Our kids hated zucchinis, our friends and
family wouldn't take any more of them, and
I couldn't bear the thought of throwing food
away. So, I thought I'd give pickling a go. And
once I'd begun, I couldn't stop.

I was intensely focused on figuring out ways
to reduce food waste on a domestic level in
a busy urban neighbourhood. I taught myself
as many traditional food skills as I could to
deal with the excess. I preserved obsessively,
putting anything I could get my hands on
into a jar. Homegrown vegetables, fruit from
neighbours' unloved trees, whatever was
cheap at the markets or was left over in the
fridge at the end of the week.

Within a year our entire garage was
filled with pickles, chutneys, sauces, jams,
marmalades and sauerkraut. Now the problem
wasn't too many zucchinis, but too many jars.
Not long after this, Jimmy and I decided to
start our family business, Cornersmith. We
opened a little café in our neighbourhood
that highlighted the way we ate at home:
assembling a variety of delicious elements.
One or two interesting vegetable dishes, a
jar of pickles or ferments, a nice loaf of bread
and a small, simple protein such as a beautiful
wedge of cheese, some boiled eggs, a grilled
piece of fish or meat. And everyone loved it.
Cornersmith was a hit!

My pickles and preserves became what
we were known for. Locals would bring in
their excess homegrown produce for me to
preserve and it would end up on the menu
later in the year. Pretty quickly we opened
a Picklery and Cooking School to share my
knowledge and skills with the community.
We opened another café, won a lot of awards,
wrote four cookbooks and spread the word
about food sustainability.

Pickling for us has come to represent much
more than just delicious condiments. While
pickling and eating pickles, we talk about
the importance of cooking from scratch and
knowing where your food comes from, share
helpful tips to reduce food waste, and teach
food history and seasonality. People are
looking for ways to connect with food and
family traditions, to be more self-sufficient
and more sustainable in the kitchen — and
pickling is an easy, approachable and delicious
way to start.

Having a pantry full of homemade pickles
and chutneys is a very satisfying feeling. They
quickly make a simple meal more interesting,
you always have a gift on hand to take to

someone's house and it is a real buzz to know that you have rescued excess food and turned it into something delicious.

Pickles are part of our everyday meals: pickled ginger tossed through some noodles with shredded chicken and coriander; a leafy green salad with pickled peaches and toasted almonds; pickled fennel with some grilled fish, rice and mayo; pickled cucumbers and cheese toasties for breakfast, lunch and dinner. A homemade onion relish turns a burger into something fancy, a quick corn salsa will make your tacos shine and a homemade hot sauce makes every dinner a little bit better.

Getting started is easy. Have a look in your fridge, fruit bowl or garden and see what needs using up. You'll need vinegar, sugar, salt, a few spices, a saucepan and a few jars. Have a good read of the how-to guides at the back of the book — you'll find information for pickling, chutney making, fermentation, jar sterilisation and heat processing. Start small and give it a go. Then the next time you're doing the shopping, grab a big bottle of vinegar and a couple of kilos of something that's cheap, abundant, in season and looking good and try your hand at making a bigger batch.

The recipes in this book will show you how to pickle and preserve everything and anything. You'll find a year's worth of projects, from quick tips on how to use up a few celery sticks or a couple of chillies, through to bigger projects where you'll make a seasonal batch

to squirrel away in the pantry. And don't forget, it's absolutely worth making one jar of pickles or a tiny batch of chutney. If you've got a few beetroot (beets) in the fridge, pickle them! Half a pumpkin (squash) lying around? Make a half batch of Pumpkin & Sesame Chutney (page 167). Use these recipes as a guide, halve them, double them, add more salt or chilli, switch out spices, substitute one vegetable for another and see what happens. Make these recipes your own once you've got the hang of it; preserving is fun, creative and addictive — the only downfall is that you might have to move your car out of the garage to make room for all your jars.

Happy pickling!

Alex -
xx

Spring

IN SEASON: Asparagus, fennel, green chilli, green mango, green tomato, jalapeño, lettuce, radish, zucchini

Pickled Green Chillies

PREPARATION TIME:
10 mins, plus 20 mins sterilising, plus 15 mins heat-processing

STORAGE: **up to 2 years**

MAKES: **2 x 500 ml (17 fl oz/2 cup) jars**

500 g (1 lb 2 oz) long green chillies, washed

2 tsp black peppercorns

2 tsp coriander, fennel or cumin seeds

500 ml (17 fl oz/2 cups) white wine vinegar

110 g (3¾ oz/½ cup) caster (superfine) sugar

2 tsp salt

250 ml (9 fl oz/1 cup) water

These chillies are amazing – and, funnily enough, they were a bit of a fluke. We found ourselves with a few extra boxes of chillies on our hands one week, so we poured a brine over them, popped them in the cool room, and proceeded to forget all about them. Six months later, we found them hiding on a high shelf and were blown away by their deliciousness! They're great on their own, in a Mexican-style salsa or a potato salad, or thinly sliced and tossed through raw salads and slaws to give them an extra kick. Try making these pickles with red chillies too.

First sterilise your jars and lids (see page 181) and allow to cool.

Pierce each chilli with a sharp knife so the brine can get inside and pickle them. Place a teaspoon of peppercorns and seeds in the bottom of each sterilised jar, then pack in the chillies (see page 179 for more on packing techniques).

Make a brine by putting the vinegar, sugar, salt and water into a small non-reactive saucepan. Place over low heat, stirring to dissolve the sugar and salt. Once the sugar and salt have completely dissolved, let the brine simmer for a few mins, then turn off the heat.

Pour the hot brine over the chillies, making sure they are completely submerged. Remove any air bubbles by gently tapping each jar on the work surface and sliding a butterknife or chopstick around the inside to release any hidden air pockets. You may need to add more chillies or brine after doing this (the liquid should reach about 1 cm/½ inch from the top of the jar). Wipe the rims of the jars with paper towel or a clean damp cloth and seal.

Heat-process the jars (see page 180) for 15 mins, then store in a cool, dark place for up to 2 years.

Quick Pickled Radishes

The prettiest pickle we make, this one works better as a quick pickle that is kept in the fridge for a week, rather than being bottled and stored for months on end. The texture of pickled radishes deteriorates quite quickly – they go rubbery and lose their colour – but this method keeps them crunchy. These can be used in salads, eaten with bread and butter, on a ploughman's plate or in light, Asian-inspired dishes.

We like to keep the tails on our radishes. If your radishes are small, keep them whole; if they're larger, halve or quarter them.

For the quick-pickling brine, put the vinegar, sugar, salt and water into a small non-reactive saucepan. Place over low heat, stirring to dissolve the sugar and salt. Once the sugar and salt have completely dissolved, add the allspice, peppercorns and bay leaves and simmer the brine for a couple of mins.

Put the radishes into a clean glass container with a lid. Pour the hot brine over them, then leave to cool before storing in the fridge for a week or so. Although these pickled radishes can be eaten the next day, their flavour is better after a few days in the fridge.

PREPARATION TIME: 20 mins

STORAGE: up to 2 weeks in the fridge

MAKES: about 750 ml (26 fl oz/3 cups)

500 ml (17 fl oz/2 cups) white wine vinegar

2 Tbsp caster (superfine) sugar

1 tsp salt

250 ml (9 fl oz/1 cup) water

4 dried allspice berries

6 black peppercorns

2 bay leaves

400 g (14 oz) radishes, about 2 bunches, washed

Soy-Pickled Lettuce

PREPARATION TIME:
15 mins, plus 10 mins
salting

STORAGE: up to 1 month
in the fridge

MAKES: 1 x 300 ml
(10½ fl oz/1¼ cup) jar

300 g (10½ oz/4 cups)
chopped cos (romaine)
or iceberg lettuce

1 Tbsp caster (superfine)
sugar

½ tsp salt

80 ml (2½ fl oz/⅓ cup) soy
sauce

1 Tbsp rice wine vinegar or
apple cider vinegar

2 tsp grated fresh ginger

pinch of chilli flakes

This is a riff on a Korean condiment and is a great way to use up excess or tired-looking lettuce. It takes only 15 mins to make and goes well with stir-fries, grilled fish, fried rice or noodles.

Put the lettuce in a bowl and sprinkle with the sugar and salt. Let it sit for 10 mins or so.

In a jug, combine the soy sauce, vinegar, grated ginger and chilli flakes. Use your hands to squeeze out the moisture from the lettuce over the sink – you can be quite rough with it!

Transfer the lettuce to a clean jar or non-reactive container and cover with the soy and vinegar mixture, pressing down the lettuce to ensure it is completely covered by the liquid.

It will be ready in 15 mins but will be even better in a few days' time.

Store in the fridge for up to 1 month.

Japanese-Style Soy-Pickled Cucumber

These pickles will be delicious in a few hours and will then last for 2–3 weeks in the fridge. We tend to use Lebanese or telegraph cucumbers, but any kind will do. Try this recipe with daikon, chopped iceberg lettuce, celery or radishes. Eat your pickles with rice and noodle dishes or dumplings.

Peel or don't peel the cucumbers, depending on how much energy you have, the state of the peel and how fancy you are. If your cucumbers are big and old, cut them in half lengthways and scoop out the seeds. Slice into rounds, cubes or wedges. Put the cucumber in a colander, sprinkle generously with salt and let sit for 15 mins or so to release excess liquid.

In a small saucepan, gently heat the soy sauce or tamari, vinegar and caster sugar. Stir to dissolve the sugar, then remove from the heat and set aside.

Pat the cucumber slices dry with paper towel or a clean tea towel (dish towel) and transfer to a clean jar or container. For extra flavour you can add a few slices of fresh ginger, chopped chilli, sliced garlic or a splash of sesame oil.

Cover with the soy mixture, pushing the cucumber down under the liquid. Seal, then swish the jar around to make sure all the cucumber is lightly coated – more liquid will form over time, so don't worry if it's not all completely covered at first. Store in the fridge for up to 2–3 weeks.

PREPARATION TIME:
20 mins, plus 15 mins salting

STORAGE: up to 2–3 weeks in the fridge

MAKES: 1 x 300 ml (10½ fl oz/1¼ cup) jar

1–2 cucumbers

½ tsp salt

60 ml (2 fl oz/¼ cup) soy sauce or tamari

2 Tbsp rice wine vinegar

1 Tbsp caster (superfine) sugar

few slices of fresh ginger (optional)

1 small chilli, chopped (optional)

1 garlic clove, sliced (optional)

splash of sesame oil (optional)

Hot Pink Turnips

PREPARATION TIME:
**20 mins, plus up to
4 days fermenting**

STORAGE: **up to 6 months**

MAKES: **2 x 500 ml
(17 fl oz/2 cup) jars**

**500 ml (17 fl oz/2 cups)
water**

2 tsp salt

**1 beetroot (beet), peeled
and cut in half**

500 g (1 lb 2 oz) turnips

This ferment was inspired by a classic Lebanese pickle. The hot pink colour comes from the beetroot – and the longer you leave the turnips to ferment, the more the colour will develop. Although there are no added spices, fermented turnips alone are surprisingly full of flavour. Feel free to tweak this to your own taste: you could add coriander seeds, fennel seeds, cleaned coriander (cilantro) roots, peppercorns (black or pink), or a whole peeled garlic clove. Serve with meats, falafel and all Middle Eastern dishes.

To make a brine, put the water and the salt in a non-reactive saucepan. Bring to the boil, then add one half of the beetroot and simmer for 2 mins. Set aside and leave the brine to cool to room temperature.

Peel the turnips and cut into strips about 6 cm x 1 cm (2½ inch x ½ inch). Cut the other half of the beetroot into 1 cm (½ inch) cubes.

When the brine and jars are both cool, pack the turnips into clean jars, adding a few cubes of beetroot to each jar (see page 179 for more on packing techniques). Remove the beetroot half from the brine, then fill the jars with the brine, making sure the vegetables are completely covered. Wipe the rims of the jars with paper towel or a clean damp cloth and seal.

Let the jars sit at room temperature (but out of direct sunlight) for 2–7 days. During this time, the lids will start to pop up, which is a sign of the fermenting process (see pages 184–185 for more details). Open your jar every few days to 'burp' your ferment – this will release the built-up carbon dioxide, and prevent brine spilling out of the jar.

Transfer the jars to the fridge and leave for a week before opening, then use within 6 months.

Green Tomato Relish

Red tomatoes aren't really at their best until summer is in full swing, so this is a great way to get your tomato relish fix in the springtime. We serve this with poached eggs, or on ham sandwiches and wraps. It's also nice on toast – put a dollop on top of fresh ricotta and sprinkle with herbs.

Put the green tomatoes into a bowl and sprinkle with the salt. Mix well and leave to sit for at least an hour – you can leave them to sit overnight if you have the time. This draws out excess moisture from the tomatoes.

Heat the vegetable oil in a large, heavy-based saucepan over medium heat. Add the ginger and spices and stir until fragrant. Add the onions and sauté for about 15 mins or until they have collapsed – you want the onions to be very soft and sweet.

Drain off any excess liquid from the salted tomatoes, then add the tomatoes to the pan and stir until well mixed. Lower the heat and cook until the tomatoes have softened, then add the sugar and vinegar, stirring to dissolve the sugar. Slowly bring to the boil, then let the relish simmer, uncovered, for about 40 mins, or until the desired consistency is reached: the relish should be glossy and thick, with no puddles of liquid on the surface.

Meanwhile, sterilise your jars and lids (see page 181).

Taste the relish and add more salt, if needed, then set aside to cool for 10 mins. Carefully ladle the hot relish into the hot jars. Wipe the rims of the jars with paper towel or a clean damp cloth, then seal and heat-process (see page 180) for 10 mins.

Leave to cool before storing in a cool, dark place for up to 12 months.

PREPARATION TIME:
20 mins, plus at least 1 hour salting (or overnight), plus 20 mins sterilising, plus 10 mins heat-processing

COOKING TIME: 1 hour

STORAGE: up to 1 year

MAKES: 4 x 300 ml (10½ fl oz/1¼ cup) jars

1.5 kg (3 lb 5 oz) green (unripe) tomatoes, cut into 1 cm (½ inch) cubes

2 Tbsp salt

60 ml (2 fl oz/¼ cup) vegetable oil or olive oil

100 g (3½ oz) fresh ginger, thinly sliced or finely grated

2 tsp brown mustard seeds

½ tsp freshly ground black pepper

1 tsp ground coriander

½ tsp ground turmeric

1 tsp ground fenugreek

1 kg (2 lb 4 oz) onions, thinly sliced

110 g (3¾ oz/½ cup) caster (superfine) sugar

500 ml (17 fl oz/2 cups) white wine vinegar

Green Tomato
Hot Sauce

PREPARATION TIME:
**20 mins, plus 20 mins
sterilising, plus 10 mins
heat-processing**

COOKING TIME: **5 mins**

STORAGE: **up to 1 year**

MAKES: **5 x 250 ml (9 fl oz/
1 cup) bottles**

**750 g (1 lb 10 oz) green
(unripe) tomatoes, roughly
chopped**

**juice and finely grated zest
of 4 limes**

**125 g (4½ oz) green
chillies, roughly chopped**

**125 g (4½ oz) onions,
roughly chopped**

**2 large garlic cloves,
roughly chopped**

**2 Tbsp caster (superfine)
sugar**

1 tsp salt

**125 ml (4 fl oz/½ cup) white
wine vinegar**

Our green tomato hot sauce is delicious and makes a great alternative to Tabasco. We use it all the time when we've made something kid-friendly that needs a lift for the adults. You can also mix it through vinaigrettes for a salad dressing. It's best to make enough to last you for the whole year. Try making a red version with red tomatoes and red chillies later in the season.

First sterilise your bottles (see page 181).

Put all the ingredients except the vinegar into a food processor and blend into a thin, smooth paste.

Pour the paste into a saucepan and add the vinegar. Bring to the boil and let it bubble for a few mins, then carefully pour into the hot sterilised bottles.

Seal and store in the fridge for 2–3 months or heat-process the bottles (see page 180) for 10 mins, then leave to cool before storing in a cool, dark place for up to 12 months.

Pickled Charred Jalapeños

You can pickle these chillies raw, or lightly char or smoke them for added flavour and sweetness. We don't generally use spices in this recipe – it's more about preserving the jalapeños when the season is in full swing, to use later in the year. However, you could add a slice of ginger, a few black peppercorns, some mustard seeds and a garlic clove to each jar. To make a simple salsa, chop a few pickled jalapeños with fresh coriander (cilantro) and red onion, then season with salt and pepper.

Lightly char the whole chillies, without using any oil. The easiest way to do this is on a barbecue or chargrill pan, or over a gas flame; this usually takes 10–15 mins. Turn the chillies regularly, so they are evenly charred and wrinkled all over. (If you have a smoker, even better – the chillies are amazing smoked and then pickled!)

Make your brine by combining the vinegar, water, sugar and salt in a non-reactive, medium-sized saucepan. Place over low heat and stir to dissolve the sugar and salt. Bring to a simmer, then turn off the heat. Meanwhile, sterilise your jars and lids (see page 181).

When the jars are cool enough to handle, put any spices you may be using in the bottom of each jar. Pack the chillies firmly into the jars, leaving about 1 cm (½ inch) space at the top.

Bring your brine back up to the boil. Pour the hot brine over the chillies, making sure they are completely submerged. You may need to pack in more chillies once they've softened in the hot brine. The more tightly packed the jars are, the less chance there is of the chillies floating and not preserving properly.

Remove any air bubbles by gently tapping each jar on the work surface and sliding a clean butterknife or chopstick around the inside to release any hidden air pockets. Wipe the rims of the jars with paper towel or a clean damp cloth and seal.

Heat-process the jars (see page 180) for 15 mins, then store in a cool, dark place for up to 2 years. Once opened, refrigerate and use within 6 months.

PREPARATION TIME: 25 mins, plus 20 mins sterilising, plus 15 mins heat-processing

COOKING TIME: 20 mins

STORAGE: up to 2 years

MAKES: 2 x 300 ml (10½ fl oz/1¼ cup) jars

500 g (1 lb 2 oz) jalapeño chillies (or any chillies of your choice), pierced with a sharp knife to allow the vinegar to seep in during pickling

350 ml (12 fl oz/scant 1½ cups) white wine vinegar

170 ml (5½ fl oz/⅔ cup) water

45 g (1½ oz/¼ cup) caster (superfine) sugar

1½ tsp salt

Delicate
Fermented Daikon

PREPARATION TIME:
**15 mins, plus 2–7 days
fermenting**

STORAGE: **up to 6 months
in the fridge**

MAKES: **1 x 500 ml
(17 fl oz/2 cup) jar**

250 ml (9 fl oz/1 cup) water

1 tsp salt

1 (250g) daikon

1 whole red chilli

1 slice of fresh ginger

Daikon was one of the first vegetables to be fermented. As it is native to Korea, the first kimchis were made with it. Eat this fermented daikon in stir-fries, in rice paper rolls, with san choy bow or in salads.

Make a brine by boiling the water with the salt in a medium saucepan, then set aside to cool to room temperature.

While the brine is cooling, wash and cut the daikon into thin matchsticks or thicker batons, depending on how you like to eat it, ensuring first that they will fit into your clean jar.

Put the daikon in the clean, empty jar, then add the chilli and a slice of ginger for a subtle heat. Fill the jar with the cooled brine, making sure the daikon is completely covered. Wipe the rim of the jar and seal.

Store your jar in a cool, dry place for 2–7 days. During this time, you'll notice that the brine begins to bubble and some may escape. Simply wipe the jar down. After 2 days, try your daikon. If you're happy with the flavour, place in the fridge. If you'd like it a little more sour, or the weather has been cold (low temperatures slow down fermentation), let it sit for up to 1 week. Open your jar every few days to 'burp' your ferment – this will release the built-up carbon dioxide, and prevent brine spilling out of the jar. Keep tasting until you're happy. (See pages 184–185 for more details about fermenting.)

Fermented daikon may be eaten immediately but will improve after 1 week in the fridge. Once the jar is open, store in the fridge for up to 6 months.

Vietnamese-Style Daikon Pickles

The area where we live in Sydney is home to a thriving Vietnamese community. We eat banh mi baguettes as often as we do cheese and pickle toasties. We owe a debt to this community for teaching us how pickles can and should accompany almost anything. The local flavour profile is sweet and sour, and a good Vietnamese pickle must strike this balance. This is the classic pickle you'll see accompanying an array of Vietnamese dishes. We're making this version with daikon only, but the classic recipe also has carrot in it. Feel free to mix them together, and to double the recipe if you've been brave and bought a giant daikon. Make your own banh mi and top generously with these pickles or use them in rice paper rolls or a cold noodle salad.

PREPARATION TIME: **10 mins**

STORAGE: **up to 1 month in the fridge**

MAKES: **1 x 500 ml (17 fl oz/2 cup) jar**

250 g (9 oz) daikon

250 ml (9 fl oz/1 cup) water

125 ml (4 fl oz/½ cup) rice wine vinegar

1 Tbsp caster (superfine) sugar

2 tsp salt

Cut the daikon into matchsticks. You want them the same shape and size, so they pickle evenly.

In a medium-sized saucepan, combine the water, rice wine vinegar, sugar and salt. Stir over medium heat to dissolve the salt and sugar completely, then allow the pickling liquid to come to the boil. Remove from the heat and cool slightly.

Pack the daikon into a clean and dry jar, then cover with the warm vinegar mixture. Seal and allow the jar to cool before transferring to the fridge.

The pickles will take 3 days to be ready and will then last for 1 month in the fridge.

Pickled Asparagus with Garlic & Lemon

PREPARATION TIME:
20 mins, plus 20 mins sterilising

STORAGE: **up to 6 months in the fridge or pantry**

MAKES: **2 x 500 ml (17 fl oz/2 cup) jars**

375 ml (13 fl oz/1½ cups) white wine vinegar

75 g (2½ oz/⅓ cup) caster (superfine) sugar

1½ tsp salt

375 ml (13 fl oz/1½ cups) water

4 thyme sprigs

4 bay leaves

4 garlic cloves, peeled

8 strips of lemon peel

1 tsp white peppercorns

about 20 asparagus spears

We make these pickles all through asparagus season in spring. They're great thinly sliced through salads, on an antipasto plate or straight out of the jar. Storing them in the fridge, rather than the cupboard, helps the asparagus retain its colour and crunch.

Sterilise your jars and lids (see page 181).

Meanwhile, make your brine by combining the vinegar, sugar, salt and water in a non-reactive, medium-sized saucepan. Place over low heat and stir to dissolve the sugar and salt. Add the thyme sprigs, bay leaves, garlic cloves, lemon peel strips and peppercorns and slowly bring to simmering point.

Wash and dry your asparagus. If the spears are long, cut in half.

When the jars are cool enough to handle, use a clean pair of tongs to put 4 lemon peel strips from the brine into each jar, along with 2 garlic cloves, 2 thyme sprigs, 2 bay leaves and ½ teaspoon of peppercorns. Now carefully pack the raw asparagus in – you should be able to get about 10 spears into each jar.

Cover the asparagus with the hot brine, making sure the asparagus is completely submerged under the vinegar. Tuck the asparagus stems down under the shoulders of the jars if you need to.

Remove any air bubbles by gently tapping each jar on the work surface and sliding a clean butterknife or chopstick around the inside to release any hidden air pockets. Wipe the rims of the jars with paper towel or a clean damp cloth and heat-process (see page 180) for 15 mins.

You can store these pickles in the cupboard for up to 6 months. We prefer not to heat-process and to keep them in the fridge, as the cold helps the asparagus spears keep their crunch; they will also last in the fridge for up to 6 months. Try to let them sit for 2–4 weeks before eating.

Pickled
Green Tomatoes

Green tomatoes – unripe red tomatoes – are our favourite spring vegetable. Tart, crunchy and delicious, they make the best pickles, and these just get better and better with time. Your friends and neighbours will love it when you share these around.

First, prepare your tomatoes. Cut any larger tomatoes into quarters or thick slices, and smaller tomatoes in half. Place in a large bowl. Mix the onion through, if using, then sprinkle with the salt. Allow to sit for 2 hours, or even overnight, to draw the excess moisture out.

Make your brine by combining the vinegar, water, sugar, salt and turmeric in a non-reactive, medium-sized saucepan over low heat. Stir to dissolve the sugar, then bring to simmering point. Let cool.

Meanwhile, sterilise your jars and lids (see page 181).

When the jars are cool enough to handle, drain off and discard the excess liquid from your tomatoes. Into each jar, put 1 cinnamon stick, 2 garlic cloves, a lemon peel strip, a bay leaf and ½ teaspoon of peppercorns. Using small clean tongs or clean hands, carefully but tightly pack the tomato pieces into the jars. Pour the brine over until the tomatoes are completely covered.

Remove any air bubbles by gently tapping each jar on the work surface and sliding a clean butterknife or chopstick around the inside to release any hidden air pockets. Wipe the rims of the jars with paper towel or a clean damp cloth and seal immediately.

Heat-process the jars (see page 180) for 15 mins, then let cool.

These pickles will keep in a cool, dark place for up to 2 years, but do let them sit for at least 1 month before you try them; they'll be even better after 3 months. Once opened, refrigerate and use within 6 months.

TIP: The garlic cloves will take on a blue–grey hue with time, in reaction to the vinegar. Blanching them in boiling water for 10 seconds before adding them to the pickling jars will stop any discolouration.

PREPARATION TIME: 20 mins, plus 2 hours salting, plus 20 mins sterilising, plus 15 mins heat-processing

STORAGE: **up to 2 years**

MAKES: **3–4 x 500 ml (17 fl oz/2 cup) jars**

1 kg (2 lb 4 oz) green (unripe) tomatoes

1 large onion, thinly sliced (optional)

1 Tbsp salt

750 ml (26 fl oz/3 cups) white wine vinegar

375 ml (13 fl oz/1½ cups) water

165 g (5¾ oz/¾ cup) caster (superfine) sugar

2 tsp salt

½ tsp ground turmeric

3–4 cinnamon sticks

6–8 garlic cloves, peeled

3–4 strips of lemon peel

3–4 bay leaves

1½–2 tsp black peppercorns

Fermented Tomatoes with Celery & Caraway

PREPARATION TIME:
15 mins, plus 1–2 hours salting, plus at least 2 days fermenting

STORAGE: **up to 6 months in the fridge**

MAKES: **2–3 x 500 ml (17 fl oz/2 cup) jars**

---

1 kg (2 lb 4 oz) green or under-ripe tomatoes, quartered

200 g (7 oz) celery stalks and leaves, chopped

2 tsp caraway seeds

2 tsp black peppercorns

2 tsp salt

These are a staple pickle on Eastern European tables. We love to eat them over spring and summer. They're great on a cheese plate, or sliced in a salad, and have even been described as vegan 'salami'! You can use completely green tomatoes, or under-ripe tomatoes that are just starting to turn red.

This version, by our resident fermenter Jaimee Edwards, was inspired by a recipe from one of her food heroes, Ukrainian chef and food writer Olia Hercules.

Toss all the ingredients together in a mixing bowl. Set aside for at least 1–2 hours to draw the moisture from the tomatoes.

Pack the mixture into clean jars, including the salty liquid that has released from the tomatoes, pressing down as you pack to release more liquid.

Once packed, the tomatoes need to be covered by about 1 cm (½ inch) of liquid; if they aren't, simply top up the jars with water.

Seal the lids, then place your jars out of direct sunlight for 2–7 days, depending on how warm the ambient temperature is. The warmer the weather, the faster your vegetables will ferment.

Open your jar every few days to 'burp' your ferment – this will release the built-up carbon dioxide, and prevent brine spilling out of the jar. Just be sure to press down your mixture afterwards, so that the brine is covering the top by at least 1 cm (½ inch). If any brine does escape, simply wipe the jar down.

After 2 days, taste your tomatoes. If you like them, place them in the fridge, where they will last for up to 6 months.

If you want to ferment your tomatoes further, keep checking and tasting every 2 days until you are happy with the flavour, then store in the fridge.

Pink Pickled Eggs

In this recipe you can also use the brine from another pickle to lightly pickle your eggs. We suggest the brine from the Pickled Rhubarb on page 131, as it gives the eggs a nice dusty pink colour; you could also use the brine from the Sweet Pickled Pears (page 164) or Malt Pickled Onions (page 151), or experiment with any other brines you have in the fridge. You'll need about 250 ml (9 fl oz/1 cup) of brine for a 500 ml (17 fl oz/ 2 cup) jar.

Boil the eggs in a saucepan of water for 9 mins; they need to be hard-boiled. Run the eggs under cool water, then carefully peel them. Place in a bowl and keep in the fridge until completely cool.

Meanwhile, make your brine by combining the vinegar, sugar, water and honey in a non-reactive, medium-sized saucepan. Place over low heat and stir to dissolve the sugar and honey. Add the spices and orange peel strips and slowly bring to simmering point. Turn off the heat and let the vinegar cool and flavours develop.

Once the eggs and the vinegar are cool, carefully pack the eggs into a clean jar, being careful not to break the whites. Pour the brine into the jar, making sure the eggs are completely submerged. Remove any air bubbles by gently tapping the jar on the work surface and sliding a clean butterknife or chopstick around the inside to release any hidden air pockets. Wipe the rim of the jar with paper towel or a clean damp cloth and seal.

Leave to sit in the fridge for at least 1 week before eating. The eggs will last for up to 3 weeks in the fridge before they start to go a bit rubbery.

PREPARATION TIME:
15 mins

COOKING TIME:
about 15 mins

STORAGE: up to 3 weeks in the fridge

MAKES: 1 x 500 ml (17 fl oz/2 cup) jar

4–5 free-range eggs, depending on size

125 ml (4 fl oz/½ cup) red wine vinegar

140 g (5 oz/⅔ cup) raw sugar

60 ml (2 fl oz/¼ cup) water

2 tsp honey

10 g (¼ oz) knob of fresh ginger, washed but not peeled, cut into slices about 1 cm (½ inch) thick

4 dried allspice berries

4 black peppercorns

2 strips of orange peel

Pickled Garlic

PREPARATION TIME:
20 mins

STORAGE: **up to 3 months
in the fridge**

MAKES: **1 x 400 ml
(14 fl oz/1½ cup) jar**

3 garlic bulbs

**300 ml (10½ fl oz) apple
cider vinegar**

**55 g (2 oz/¼ cup) caster
(superfine) sugar**

pinch of salt

pinch of ground turmeric

2 bay leaves

½ tsp peppercorns

The jars of minced garlic in supermarkets are full of additives and taste nothing like garlic should. This is our version, although we leave the cloves whole and mince them as needed.

Break up the garlic and blanch the unpeeled cloves in a saucepan of boiling water for 1 min (this is to prevent the garlic turning blue in the vinegar). Drain and run under cold water, then peel the cloves.

In a jug, combine the apple cider vinegar, sugar, salt and turmeric. Whisk until dissolved.

Fill a clean jar with the peeled garlic cloves, adding the bay leaves and peppercorns. Cover with the pickling liquid, making sure the cloves are submerged. Remove any air bubbles by gently tapping each jar on the work surface and sliding a butterknife or chopstick around the inside, then seal and store in the fridge for up to 3 months.

Garlic Oxymel

Oxymels are a combination of vinegar and honey, together with an ingredient that has medicinal properties. Traditionally, it was a way of making medicine easier to take, and frankly it still is. Garlic has been valued for its health benefits for thousands of years. It has anti-inflammatory, antibiotic and antihistamine properties, can help lower cholesterol and blood pressure, and can also support the liver in detoxifying the body. But chomping on cloves of raw garlic is pretty rough, so make this concoction and take your daily dose pleasantly.

In a clean and dry jar, mix the apple cider vinegar with the honey, then add the chopped garlic cloves. Set aside on the benchtop to infuse for 1–2 weeks, then keep in the fridge for up to 6 months.

Add 1 tablespoon to hot water for a morning tea or take a spoonful to help fight off cold symptoms or when feeling run down.

PREPARATION TIME:
10 mins, plus 1–2 weeks infusing

STORAGE: up to 6 months in the fridge

MAKES: 80 ml (2½ fl oz/ ⅓ cup)

60 ml (2 fl oz/¼ cup) apple cider vinegar

3 Tbsp raw honey

4–5 garlic cloves, chopped

Quick Pickled
Red Onions

PREPARATION TIME:
**15 mins, plus 30 mins
salting**

STORAGE: **up to 1 month
in the fridge**

MAKES: **1 x 500 ml
(17 fl oz/2 cup) jar
or container**

**375 ml (13 fl oz/1½ cups)
red wine vinegar**

**110 g (3¾ oz/½ cup) raw
sugar**

**1 tsp salt, plus extra for
sprinkling over the onions**

125 ml (4 fl oz/½ cup) water

2 cloves

½ tsp fennel seeds

½ tsp cumin seeds

½ tsp chilli flakes

**300 g (10½ oz) red onion,
thinly sliced**

These quick and easy pickled onions are great tossed through salads, and on tortillas and burgers. Make them for your next barbecue and everyone will be very impressed that you pickle. They'll last for several weeks in the fridge.

Make your brine by combining the vinegar, sugar, salt and water in a non-reactive, medium-sized saucepan. Place over low heat and stir to dissolve the sugar and salt. Add the spices and chilli flakes and slowly bring to simmering point. Turn the heat off and let the brine cool and the flavours develop a little.

Meanwhile, put the onion in a clean jar or non-reactive container. Sprinkle with a little extra salt and leave to sit for 30 mins or so, to draw out the excess moisture.

Drain off and discard the excess liquid from the onion slices. Pour the room-temperature brine over the onion, making sure all the slices are submerged.

Cover and store in the fridge for up to 1 month.

Turmeric Pickled Mango

So addictive are these pickles, you'll be lucky if they make it past the first meal. They are delicious with curries or mixed through Asian-style salads. For a quick salsa to serve with seafood or tacos, finely dice some of the pickled mango and mix in a small amount of the brine, lots of fresh chopped coriander (cilantro) and fresh chilli to taste.

Peel the mangoes, then cut the flesh into long strips about 1 cm (½ inch) thick. Place in a bowl and sprinkle with the salt. Mix with your hands to evenly coat, then leave to sit for at least an hour, to draw the excess moisture out.

Meanwhile, in a dry frying pan, lightly toast all the spices over medium heat for 1–2 mins, or until fragrant, taking care not to burn the fenugreek seeds or they will become bitter.

Make your brine by combining the vinegar, sugar and water in a non-reactive, medium-sized saucepan. Place over low heat and stir to dissolve the sugar, then bring to simmering point. Turn off the heat and allow to cool a little.

Drain off and discard the excess liquid from your mango strips; you can wrap them in paper towel to absorb more moisture.

Put 2 curry leaves and 2 teaspoons of your toasted spice mixture into the bottom of each clean jar. Carefully pack in the mango strips. They will have become soft from the salting; get as much as you can into each jar, without squashing or breaking up the mango strips.

Cover with the brine, making sure the mango strips are completely submerged under the liquid.

Remove any air bubbles by gently tapping each jar on the work surface and sliding a clean butterknife or chopstick around the inside to release any hidden air pockets. Wipe the rims of the jars with paper towel or a clean damp cloth and seal immediately.

Keep these pickles in the fridge as the texture deteriorates quite quickly. They're best eaten within 3 months.

PREPARATION TIME:
25 mins, plus 1 hour salting

STORAGE: up to 3 months in the fridge

MAKES: 3 x 500 ml (17 fl oz/2 cup) jars

2 kg (4 lb 8 oz) unripe mangoes, or green mangoes

1½ Tbsp salt

1 tsp fenugreek seeds

1 tsp fennel seeds

1 tsp cumin seeds

½ tsp ground turmeric

1 tsp yellow mustard powder

1 tsp chilli flakes

400 ml (14 fl oz/generous 1½ cups) white wine vinegar

110 g (3¾ oz/½ cup) caster (superfine) sugar

400 ml (14 fl oz/generous 1½ cups) water

6 curry leaves

Fermented Vegetables

PREPARATION TIME:
20 mins, plus 2 days to several weeks fermenting

STORAGE: **up to 6 months in the fridge**

MAKES: **1–2 x 500 ml (17 fl oz/2 cup) jars**

Jaimee Edwards teaches all of our fermenting workshops, and here is her master recipe for brining vegetables. Start with some of the spring vegetables we've suggested here, then experiment with what you have in the fridge or growing in the garden. Fermented vegetables prepared in this way are delicious in salads and on sandwiches – or to eat straight out of the jar.

2 tsp salt

500 ml (17 fl oz/2 cups) water

500 g (1 lb 2 oz) vegetables, such as green (unripe) tomatoes, gherkin cucumbers, carrots, rhubarb stalks, fennel, radishes, green chillies

Make your salt brine by combining the salt and water in a non-reactive, medium-sized saucepan. Place over low heat and stir to dissolve the salt. Bring to the boil, then turn off the heat and allow to cool to room temperature. (In fermenting, never use excessive heat, as this will kill the good bacteria we want to encourage.)

Cut your produce into whatever sizes and shapes you like – remembering that the larger the pieces, the longer they will take to fully ferment.

Pack the vegetables into clean jars, to about 1 cm (½ inch) from the top. Pour in your cooled salt brine so that it covers your produce by a few millimetres (⅛ inch). Remove any air bubbles by gently tapping each jar on the work surface and sliding a butterknife or chopstick around the inside to release any hidden air pockets. Wipe the rim of the jars with paper towel or a clean damp cloth and seal.

Place your jars out of direct sunlight so the vegetables can begin to ferment. After 2 days, check your ferment to see if the vegetables are at a stage you like. The longer you leave them, the more the flavours will develop. You can leave them to ferment for up to 3 weeks.

Open your jars every few days to 'burp' your ferment – this will release the built-up carbon dioxide and prevent brine spilling out of the jars. Just be sure to press down your vegetables afterwards, so that the brine is covering the top.

When your ferments are ready, store them in the refrigerator and eat within 6 months.

Quick Kitchen-Scrap Pickle

PREPARATION TIME:
15 mins, plus 20 mins cooling

STORAGE: **up to 2 weeks in the fridge**

MAKES: **1 x 500 ml (17 fl oz/2 cup) container**

125 ml (4 fl oz/½ cup) white wine vinegar, rice wine vinegar, apple cider vinegar or red wine vinegar

250 ml (9 fl oz/1 cup) very hot water

2–3 Tbsp caster (superfine) sugar

2 tsp salt

1 cup thinly sliced vegetables of your choice

1 tsp spices of your choice, or a few slices of fresh ginger, chilli or a bay leaf

Quick pickling is a great way to use up any vegetables in the fridge at the end of the week, as well as those leftover veggie stems – cauliflower, beetroot (beet), broccoli and kale stems all make really delicious pickles! And it's so simple: no need to worry about sterilising jars and lids.

These pickles need to be kept in the fridge and will last for about 2 weeks in an airtight jar or sealed container.

If you have any leftover brine from the bottom of other jars of pickles, you can gently heat it up in a small saucepan and use it for quick pickling, following the same method.

To make the brine, combine the vinegar, hot water, sugar and salt in a jug. Stir until the sugar and salt have dissolved.

Put your vegetables and your spices into a clean non-reactive container. Mix together well. Pour the hot brine over the vegetables and leave to sit for at least 20 mins.

Once cooled, cover and store in the fridge. The pickles will last for up to 2 weeks.

Pickled Ginger

PREPARATION TIME:
15 mins, plus 30 mins salting

STORAGE: **up to 1 year in the fridge**

MAKES: **50–100g (1¾– 3½ oz)**

small knob of fresh ginger

½ tsp salt

125 ml (4 fl oz/½ cup) rice wine vinegar

2 Tbsp caster (superfine) or white (granulated) sugar

Make your own pickled ginger, take it with you to the sushi train (conveyor-belt sushi) and pay no mind to those who might think you a little eccentric.

Thinly slice the ginger, sprinkle generously with salt and let it sit for at least 30 mins. Pat dry with paper towel or a clean tea towel (dish towel) and pop into a container or clean jar.

In a small saucepan, heat the rice wine vinegar and sugar. Once the syrup is hot and the sugar has dissolved, pour it over the ginger slices.

Seal tightly, allow to cool, then store in the fridge for up to 1 year.

Odd-Knobs
Ginger Paste

This little recipe is indispensable for using up kitchen scraps. It packs a punch and can be used as the base for a curry or laksa, stirred into yoghurt for a quick marinade or added to a noodle dish or fried rice.

Gather up all those old knobs of ginger, wash them (don't bother peeling unless they're really old and gnarly) and throw them into a food processor with your mixture of garlic, onion, chilli, carrot, celery and herb stems. Give it a good blitz, then add the salt and blitz again to make a paste.

Transfer to a clean, dry container and keep refrigerated for up to 1 month. You could add a layer of neutral oil on the surface to help the ginger paste last even longer – about 2 months in the fridge.

PREPARATION TIME:
15 mins

STORAGE: **up to 1 month in the fridge, or 2 months if covered with oil**

MAKES: **200 ml (7 fl oz)**

odd knobs of fresh ginger

200 g (7 oz) garlic, onion, chilli, carrot, celery and herb stems (make up this amount with whatever you have)

2 tsp salt

neutral oil, for storing (optional)

TIP: Next time you sauté onions, add 1–2 tablespoons of the ginger paste and let your tastebuds sing.

Pickled
Roasted Fennel

PREPARATION TIME:
25 mins, plus 20 mins
sterilising, plus at least
2 hours salting, plus
15 mins heat-processing
(optional)

COOKING TIME: 45 mins

STORAGE: up to 1 month
in the fridge, or 1 year if
heat-processed

MAKES: 1–2 x 500 ml
(17 fl oz/2 cup) jars

fennel bulbs, about 500 g
(1 lb 2 oz) in total

1 onion

80 ml (2½ fl oz/⅓ cup)
vegetable oil or olive oil

1 tsp fennel seeds

1 tsp salt

300 ml (10½ fl oz/scant
1¼ cups) white wine
vinegar

150 ml (5 fl oz/generous
½ cup) water

55 g (2 oz/¼ cup) caster
(superfine) sugar

2 garlic cloves, peeled

½ tsp black peppercorns

2 bay leaves

This is more of an antipasto-style pickle. It's so delicious you'll probably just eat it straight out of the jar, but it is lovely with soft cheeses or as part of a tasting plate for lunch. You could also serve it as a side with grilled fish or tossed through leafy salads.

Preheat the oven to 180°C (350°F). Slice the fennel into long wedges and thinly slice the onion. Put the vegetables in a baking dish. Drizzle with the oil, sprinkle with the fennel seeds and salt and mix together.

Roast for 30–45 mins, or until the fennel is soft, sweet and starting to brown on the edges.

Meanwhile, sterilise your jars and lids (see page 181).

Make your brine by combining the vinegar, water and sugar in a non-reactive, medium-sized saucepan. Place over low heat and stir to dissolve the sugar. Increase the heat and bring to the boil.

When the jars are cool enough to handle, put 1 garlic clove, a few peppercorns and 1 bay leaf into the bottom of each jar. Use a pair of small clean tongs or clean hands to carefully pack the roasted fennel and onion into the jars. Cover with the hot brine, making sure the vegetables are completely submerged.

Remove any air bubbles by gently tapping each jar on the work surface and sliding a clean butterknife or chopstick around the inside to release any hidden air pockets. Wipe the rims of the jars with paper towel or a clean damp cloth and seal immediately.

Leave to cool on the benchtop, then store in the fridge for up to 1 month. To extend the shelf life to 1 year, heat-process the jars (see page 180) for 15 mins. Once opened, refrigerate and use within 3 months.

Pickled Fennel with Chilli

We use this on sandwiches with salami, chilli and ricotta, tossed through salads – especially potato salad – or with barbecued fish.

Once you've finished eating the pickles, keep the jar of brine in the fridge. Whisked with some extra virgin olive oil, it makes a great salad dressing.

First, sterilise your jars and lids (see page 181).

Cut the fennel into long thin strips – you can use all of it, including the core, stems and fronds. Mix the fennel and onion together in a bowl. Sprinkle with the spices and toss with your hands to mix.

Make a brine by putting the vinegar, sugar, salt and water into a non-reactive saucepan over low heat. Stir to dissolve the sugar, then increase the heat and bring to the boil. Let it bubble for 1 min, then remove from the heat.

When the jars are cool enough to handle, use small tongs or clean hands to carefully pack the fennel mixture into the jars. The jars should be full but not over-packed – the brine needs to cover every strip of fennel, and if they are packed too tightly the brine won't be able to get into every nook and cranny (see page 179 for more on packing techniques).

Carefully fill the jars with the hot brine until the fennel is completely covered. Remove any air bubbles by gently tapping each jar on the work surface and sliding a butterknife or chopstick around the inside to release any hidden air pockets. You may need to add more brine or fennel after doing this (the liquid should reach about 1 cm/½ inch from the top of the jar). Wipe the rims of the jars with paper towel or a clean damp cloth and seal.

Heat-process the jars (see page 180) for 15 mins, then store in a cool, dark place for up to 12 months. Let the jars of pickled fennel mature for a few weeks before opening them, then keep in the fridge and use within 3 months.

PREPARATION TIME: 45 mins, plus 15 mins heat-processing

STORAGE: up to 1 year

MAKES: 2 x 500 ml (17 fl oz/2 cup) jars

2 large fennel bulbs

1 brown onion, sliced

1 tsp yellow mustard seeds

1 tsp chilli flakes or chopped fresh red chilli

1 tsp fennel seeds

500 ml (17 fl oz/2 cups) white wine vinegar

110 g (3¾ oz/½ cup) caster (superfine) sugar

1 tsp salt

250 ml (9 fl oz/1 cup) water

Zucchini Pickle with Chilli & Mint

PREPARATION TIME:
30 mins, plus 2 hours
salting, plus 20 mins
sterilising, plus 10 mins
heat-processing

STORAGE: up to 2 years

MAKES: 6 x 375 ml
(13 fl oz/1½ cup) jars

2 kg (4 lb 8 oz) small firm
zucchini (courgettes)

2 small brown onions

2 Tbsp salt, plus 1 tsp
for the brine

1 litre (35 fl oz/4 cups)
white wine vinegar

500 ml (17 fl oz/2 cups)
water

110 g (3¾ oz/½ cup) caster
(superfine) sugar

3 tsp dried mint

3 tsp mustard seeds

2 tsp chilli flakes (optional)

2–3 peppercorns per jar

We serve these everywhere you'd use a classic bread and butter pickle. You can leave the chilli out or add more if you like your pickles hot. Be sure you don't overpack the jars. If you squish in too much zucchini (courgette), the excess moisture will be released and make your brine too watery to preserve properly. Once you've eaten the pickles, save the brine to use in salad dressings – just whisk in olive oil and cracked black pepper.

Thinly slice the zucchini to the thickness of a coin and put in a large bowl. Thinly slice the onions and mix through the zucchini. Sprinkle with 2 tablespoons of salt and let sit for at least 2 hours to draw out any excess liquid; the larger the zucchini, the longer it will need to sit. Transfer to a colander and let sit until the liquid has drained out.

Sterilise your jars and lids (see page 181).

Make your brine by combining the vinegar, water, sugar and 1 teaspoon of salt in a non-reactive, medium-sized saucepan. Place over low heat and stir to dissolve the sugar. Increase the heat and bring to the boil.

Put the onion and zucchini slices in a large bowl. Add the mint and spices, mixing with your hand to evenly disperse them.

When the jars are cool enough to handle, use a pair of small clean tongs or clean hands to carefully pack the zucchini mixture into them, so that each jar is full but not overpacked. Remember the brine needs to cover every slice of zucchini, and if they are packed too tightly the brine cannot coat them evenly. Slowly fill the jars with hot brine until the vegetables are completely covered.

Remove any air bubbles by gently tapping each jar on the work surface and sliding a clean butterknife or chopstick around the inside to release any hidden air pockets. Wipe the rims of the jars with paper towel or a clean damp cloth and seal.

Heat-process the jars (see page 180) for 10 mins, then store in a cool, dark place for up to 2 years. Once opened, refrigerate and use within 6 months.

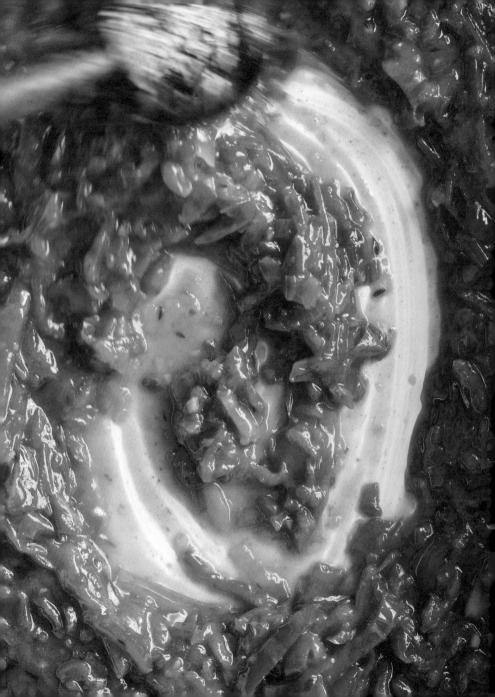

Summer

IN SEASON: Capsicum, cherries, chilli, corn, cucumber, eggplant, green beans, mango, peach, pineapple, plum, tomato, watermelon

Tomato & Eggplant Chutney

PREPARATION TIME:
30 mins, plus at least
1 hour salting, plus 20 mins
sterilising, plus 10 mins
heat-processing

COOKING TIME: 2¾ hours

STORAGE: up to 1 year

MAKES: 8 x 300 ml
(10½ fl oz/1¼ cup) jars

2 kg (4 lb 8 oz) tomatoes

2 Tbsp salt

2 kg (4 lb 8 oz) eggplants
(aubergines)

250 ml (9 fl oz/1 cup)
olive oil

3 Tbsp coriander seeds

2 Tbsp fenugreek seeds

2 Tbsp cumin seeds

1 Tbsp freshly ground
black pepper

1 tsp cayenne pepper

1 tsp chilli flakes (optional)

1 kg (2 lb 4 oz) thinly sliced
brown onion

220 g (7¾ oz/1 cup) caster
(superfine) sugar

500 ml (17 fl oz/2 cups) red
wine vinegar

Eggplants (aubergines) and tomatoes are plentiful and very cheap in the middle of summer, so make the most of them!

Cut the tomatoes into 2 cm (¾ inch) cubes and put them into a large colander set over a bowl. Sprinkle the salt over the tomatoes and mix through, then leave to sit for at least 1 hour.

Meanwhile, preheat the oven to 220°C (425°F) and line a roasting tin with baking paper. Prick the eggplants with a fork or skewer and rub with some of the olive oil. Place in the tin and roast for 45 mins or until the eggplants are soft and wrinkled. When the roasted eggplants are cool enough to handle, cut into 4 cm (1½ inch) chunks and set aside.

Use a spice grinder or pestle and mortar to grind the coriander, fenugreek and cumin to a powder, then stir in the pepper, cayenne and chilli. Pour the remaining olive oil into a large saucepan over medium heat, then add the spices and sauté until fragrant. Add the onion and sauté gently until completely soft; don't let it brown.

Pour away any liquid that has seeped from the eggplants, then add the tomatoes and eggplants to the pan. Stir well to make sure nothing is sticking, then turn down the heat and simmer for 15 mins to soften the tomatoes and eggplants. Add the sugar and vinegar and stir until the sugar has completely dissolved. Cook over low to medium heat, uncovered, for 1½ hours or until the chutney is thick and glossy, with no puddles of liquid on the surface. (If you draw a spoon through it, you should quickly see the bottom of the pan.)

When the chutney is close to being ready, sterilise your jars and lids (see page 181).

Take the chutney off the heat and let it sit for a few mins, then fill the hot jars with the hot chutney. Remove any air bubbles by gently tapping each jar on the work surface and sliding a butterknife or chopstick around the inside. Heat-process the jars (see page 180) for 10 mins, then store in a cool, dark place for up to 12 months. Once opened, refrigerate and use within 2 months.

Bread & Butter
Cucumber Pickles

These are the first pickles we ever made, and were our bestsellers. Small cucumbers are best for pickling as their water content is lower. Feel free to experiment with spices. These are classic pickle spices, but you could use whole chillies, garlic cloves, bay leaves and strips of lemon zest.

Slice the cucumbers into rounds the thickness of a coin. Put into a bowl and mix with 2 tablespoons salt, then let sit for 1–2 hours (or overnight) to draw out any excess liquid; the bigger the cucumbers, the longer it will take. Transfer to a colander and let drain.

Meanwhile, sterilise your jars and lids (see page 181).

Make a brine by putting the vinegar, sugar, turmeric, salt and water into a non-reactive, medium-sized saucepan over low heat. Stir to dissolve the sugar, then increase the heat and bring to a boil.

Transfer the cucumber to a large bowl. Add the onion, along with the mustard, fennel and dill seeds, and the chilli flakes, if using. Use your hands to mix everything together well.

When the jars are cool enough to handle, use small tongs or clean hands to carefully pack the cucumbers into the jars, adding 2 or 3 peppercorns to each jar. The jars should be full but not over-packed – the brine needs to cover every slice of cucumber, and if they are packed too tightly the brine won't be able to get into every nook and cranny (see page 179 for more on packing techniques).

Fill the jars with brine until the cucumbers are covered. Remove any air bubbles by gently tapping each jar on the work surface and sliding a butterknife or chopstick around the inside to release any hidden air pockets. You may then need to add more brine or cucumbers (the liquid should reach 1 cm/½ inch from the top of the jar). Wipe the rims of the jars with paper towel or a clean damp cloth and seal.

Heat-process the jars (see page 180) for 10 mins, then store in a cool, dark place. Although these pickles will keep for up to 12 months, they start to lose their crunch after about 6 months.

PREPARATION TIME:
20 mins, plus 1–2 hours salting, plus 20 mins sterilising, plus 10 mins heat-processing

STORAGE: up to
6–12 months

MAKES: about 6 x 375 ml
(13 fl oz/1½ cup) jars

2 kg (4 lb 8 oz) Lebanese (short) cucumbers – the smaller, the better

2 Tbsp salt, plus 1 tsp salt for the brine

1 litre (35 fl oz/4 cups) white wine vinegar

110 g (3¾ oz/½ cup) caster (superfine) sugar

½ tsp ground turmeric

500 ml (17 fl oz/2 cups) water

2 small brown onions, thinly sliced

3 tsp brown mustard seeds

2 tsp fennel seeds

2 tsp dill seeds

2 tsp chilli flakes (optional)

12–18 black peppercorns

Quick Pickled Sweetcorn Salsa

PREPARATION TIME:
15 mins

COOKING TIME: **10 mins**

STORAGE: **up to 1 week in the fridge**

MAKES: **about 300 g (10½ oz)**

200 g (7 oz/1 cup) sweetcorn kernels (2–3 cobs)

20 g (¾ oz/⅓ cup) spring onions (scallions) or red onion, thinly sliced

1–2 long green chillies or jalapeños, thinly sliced

1 Tbsp vegetable oil

3 Tbsp white wine or rice wine vinegar

1 Tbsp caster (superfine) sugar

½ tsp salt

1 tsp cumin seeds

a pinch of cayenne pepper (optional)

Taco Tuesdays step up a notch with this tangy sweetcorn salsa. It's also great with eggs and cornbread, baked fish and salad or with guacamole and corn chips.

In a bowl, combine the sweetcorn kernels, spring onion (or red onion) and the chillies. Heat the oil in a frying pan over medium–high heat. Add the corn mixture in two batches and cook, stirring, for 1–2 mins – you want to quickly char the ingredients rather than completely cook them through. Once both batches are charred, return everything to the pan and add the vinegar, sugar, salt and cumin seeds. Cook over medium heat for 2–3 mins, until the corn has absorbed most of the vinegar. Taste and add more salt or a pinch of cayenne pepper if it needs more heat.

Allow to cool and either serve straight away or store in a sealed jar or airtight container in the fridge for up to 1 week.

Fermented Chilli Paste

Fermented chilli pastes and sauces have a vibrancy and complexity that goes well beyond their heat. They need a bit more care in the fermenting process, but it is well worth the effort.

Put the red chillies, garlic, ginger, salt and sugar into a food processor. Pulse until you have a thick paste with a little texture.

Transfer to a clean jar, top with the water and seal with a lid (see pages 184–185 for further instructions on fermenting). Leave at room temperature for 3–7 days, opening the jar every second day to let out any carbon dioxide building up inside. Once it tastes spicy and mildly sour, store it in the fridge, where it will keep for up to 6 months.

PREPARATION TIME:
20 mins, plus 3–7 days fermenting

STORAGE: up to 6 months in the fridge

MAKES: 1 x 250 ml (9 fl oz/ 1 cup) jar

200 g (7 oz) long red chillies, roughly chopped

3 garlic cloves, roughly chopped

3 cm (1¼ inch) piece of fresh ginger, roughly chopped

¼ tsp salt

¼ tsp caster (superfine) sugar

1 Tbsp water

Dilly Beans

PREPARATION TIME:
30 mins, plus 20 mins
sterilising, plus 15 mins
heat-processing

STORAGE: **up to 2 years**

MAKES: **2–3 x 500 ml
(17 fl oz/2 cup) jars**

1 kg (2 lb 4 oz) hand-
picked, good-quality
green beans

750 ml (26 fl oz/3 cups)
white wine vinegar

375 ml (13 fl oz/1½ cups)
water

110 g (3¾ oz/½ cup) caster
(superfine) sugar

¼ tsp ground turmeric

2 tsp salt

FOR EACH JAR,
YOU WILL NEED:

¼ tsp black peppercorns

½ tsp dill seeds

¼ tsp dried dill

1 small red chilli or garlic
clove (optional)

fennel flowers (optional)

These pickled beans are surprisingly delicious – and they get better with age, so although they're good to eat after a month or so, try to let them sit for as long as you can wait. The best ones we had sat for about 8 months before we opened them. Just remember that the spices will intensify over time, so go easy on the chilli if you're planning on letting them sit for a while. If you grow dill or fennel at home, let some go to seed and add the flowers too.

Serve these with cold meats, chopped through a salad, or eat straight out of the jar.

Wash the green beans and trim off any blemished ends. We like to leave the beans whole and with their stems intact, as it saves time and they look very pretty in the jar.

Sterilise your jars and lids (see page 181).

Put the vinegar and water in a non-reactive, medium-sized saucepan over low heat. Add the sugar, turmeric and salt and stir to dissolve, then increase the heat and bring to the boil. Let it bubble for 2–3 mins, then remove from the heat.

When the jars are cool enough to handle, add the peppercorns, dill seeds, dried dill, chilli or garlic clove and fennel flowers, if using. Carefully pack the beans vertically in the jars (see page 179 for more on packing techniques), then pour in enough hot brine to completely cover the beans. Remove any air bubbles by gently tapping each jar on the work surface and sliding a butterknife or chopstick around the inside to release any hidden air pockets. You may need to add more brine or beans after doing this (the liquid should reach about 1 cm/½ inch from the top of the jar). Wipe the rims of the jars with paper towel or a clean damp cloth and seal.

Heat-process the jars (see page 180) for 15 mins, then leave in a cool, dark place for a month before using. Unopened jars will last for up to 2 years; once opened, refrigerate and use within 3 months.

Mango Chutney

When mangoes are cheap or you have a neighbourhood mango tree that is dropping fruit faster than you can eat it, make this chutney! It's delicious with curries and seafood and makes a great gift. This one has a bit of heat to it, but you can leave the chilli flakes out if you're after something milder.

Cut the mangoes into 3 cm (1¼ inch) pieces and discard the peel and stones. Very thinly slice the onions.

Measure out the spices and set aside.

Heat the oil in a large non-reactive saucepan. Add the onion and sauté with the salt over medium–low heat for about 8 mins, until soft and collapsed. Add the spices and stir for a minute or two, until fragrant.

Add the mango and stir until the spices are evenly mixed through. Add the vinegar and sugar, stirring to dissolve the sugar.

Cook over low heat, stirring regularly to make sure the chutney isn't sticking, for up to 1 hour, or until the chutney is glossy and thick, with no puddles of liquid on the surface. Taste and add more spices or salt if needed, then turn off the heat and leave to cool for a minute or two.

Meanwhile, sterilise your jars and lids (see page 181), putting the jars in the oven about 15 mins before the chutney has finished cooking.

Fill the hot jars with the hot chutney. Remove any air bubbles by gently tapping each jar on the work surface and sliding a clean butterknife around the inside to release any hidden air pockets. Wipe the rims of the jars with paper towel or a clean damp cloth and seal immediately.

Leave to cool on the benchtop, then store in a cool, dark place for up to 3 months. To extend the shelf life to 2 years, heat-process the jars (see page 180) for 10 mins.

Try to let the chutney sit for 1 month before you eat it. Once opened, refrigerate and use within 3 months.

PREPARATION TIME: 20 mins, plus 20 mins sterilising, plus 10 mins heat processing (optional)

COOKING TIME: about 1¼ hours

STORAGE: up to 3 months, or up to 2 years if heat-processed

MAKES: 4 x 300 ml (10½ fl oz/1¼ cup) jars

1.8–2 kg (4 lb–4 lb 8 oz) sweet, ripe mangoes; you'll need about 1.2 kg (2 lb 10 oz) sliced mango

1 brown onion

1 red onion

80 ml (2½ fl oz/⅓ cup) olive, sunflower or vegetable oil

2 tsp salt

1 tsp yellow mustard seeds

1 tsp brown mustard seeds

1 tsp ground coriander

1½ tsp ground ginger

1 tsp chilli flakes

¼ tsp cayenne pepper

300 ml (10½ fl oz/1¼ cups) apple cider vinegar

110 g (3¾ oz/½ cup) caster (superfine) sugar

Fermented Pineapple & Chilli Sambal

PREPARATION TIME:
30 mins, plus 2–7 days fermenting

STORAGE: **up to 6 months**

MAKES: **about 2 x 500 ml (17 fl oz/2 cup) jars**

2 kg (4 lb 8 oz) pineapple (about 2 medium-sized pineapples)

large handful (1 cup) coriander (cilantro) leaves, chopped

2 tsp finely grated lime zest

1 Tbsp lime juice

1 Tbsp finely grated fresh ginger

2 tsp chilli flakes or sliced fresh chilli

2 Tbsp salt

This fruit ferment comes from Sri Lanka, and it's sweet, spicy and salty. The pineapple, lime, coriander (cilantro) and ginger all retain their fresh flavour. We'd suggest serving it with seafood.

Peel the pineapples, then cut into 2 cm (¾ inch) cubes, discarding the tough core. Place the pineapple in a non-reactive bowl, then add all the other ingredients. Using your hands, squish everything together and mix thoroughly.

Pack the pineapple mixture tightly into clean jars (see page 179 for more on packing techniques), pressing down so that the juice rises above the pineapple and any air bubbles are released. Wipe the rims of the jars with paper towel or a clean damp cloth and seal.

Let the jars sit at room temperature (but out of direct sunlight) for 2–7 days. During this time, the lids will start to pop up, which is a sign of the fermenting process (see pages 184–185 for more details). Open your jar every few days to 'burp' your ferment – this will release the built-up carbon dioxide, and prevent brine spilling out of the jar.

Transfer the jars to the fridge and leave for a week before opening, then use within 6 months.

Chilli Sambal

We make mountains of this sambal when chilli season is in full swing. So quick and easy to make, it gives tacos, rice dishes, marinades and breakfast eggs a good hit of heat.

We use carrot as a base in this recipe as it adds sweetness and gives the sambal a fantastically bright colour, but you could experiment with other bases such as green mango or pineapple. Try green or yellow chillies too.

With fruit-based sambals, you may need to add more vinegar to loosen them. Keep tasting and adjusting the sugar to salt ratio until you're happy with the flavour.

Sterilise your jars and lids (see page 181).

Roughly chop the chillies, carrot, ginger and garlic. Put them in a food processor with the sugar and salt and blitz for 5 mins. Slowly pour in the vinegar until your sambal has a smooth consistency; you may need to adjust the quantity.

When the jars are cool enough to handle, pack the sambal into the jars, pressing down firmly to make sure the chilli paste is covered in a thin layer of liquid.

Remove any air bubbles by gently tapping each jar on the work surface and sliding a clean butterknife or chopstick around the inside to release any hidden air pockets. Wipe the rims of the jars with paper towel or a clean damp cloth and seal immediately.

You can store the sambal in the fridge for up to 3 months, or heat-process the jars (see page 180) for 10 mins and store in a cool, dark place for up to 2 years.

Once opened, refrigerate and use within 3 months.

PREPARATION TIME:
20 mins, plus 20 mins sterilising, plus 10 mins heat-processing (optional)

STORAGE: **up to 3 months in the fridge, or 2 years if heat-processed**

MAKES: **4–5 x 375 ml (13 fl oz/1½ cup) jars**

---

750 g (1 lb 10 oz) long mild red chillies

250 g (9 oz) carrot

50 g (1¾ oz) knob of fresh ginger

4 garlic cloves

55 g (2 oz/¼ cup) caster (superfine) sugar

1 Tbsp salt

185 ml (6 fl oz/¾ cup) white wine vinegar

TIP: If your chillies are extra hot or if you prefer your sambal milder, you can always change the ratio. Try 500 g (1 lb 2 oz) carrot to 500 g chillies – or even 750 g (1 lb 10 oz) carrot to 250 g (9 oz) chillies.

WE WANT TO GIVE YOU THE CONFIDENCE AND
INSPIRATION TO MAKE VEGETABLES THE HEROES
OF YOUR PLATE AND PANTRY. AND WE WANT TO
SHOW YOU HOW TO GET CREATIVE BY TURNING
EXCESS FROM THE FRIDGE, FRUITBOWL AND
GARDEN INTO TASTY COMPONENTS OF YOUR
EVERYDAY MEALS.

Chow Chow

PREPARATION TIME:
20 mins

COOKING TIME: 45 mins

STORAGE: up to 1–2 months
in the fridge, or 1 year
if heat-processed

MAKES: 3–4 x 300 ml
(10½ fl oz/1¼ cup) jars

2 Tbsp neutral oil

1 onion, diced

3 garlic cloves, diced

1 green or red capsicum
(pepper), diced

3 tsp mustard seeds

2 Tbsp mustard powder

a good pinch of turmeric

¼ tsp cayenne pepper

1 tsp of your favourite
ground spice (cumin,
allspice, ginger)

2 tsp salt

75 g (2½ oz/1 cup)
shredded cabbage

kernels from 4 corn cobs,
about 650 g (1 lb 7 oz)

375 ml (13 fl oz/1½ cups)
white wine vinegar

110 g (3¾ oz/½ cup) white
(granulated) sugar

125 ml (4 fl oz/½ cup) water

Chow chow is a Southern US–style relish. We like it because it's really tasty, obviously, but it's also one of those recipes where you can swap ingredients here and there. We've taken quite a few liberties with the method, but it's all been in the name of making the process easier and more delicious. Chow chow is served with barbecued meats, hot dogs, burgers, fishcakes, ham and cheese sandwiches and even mashed potatoes.

Heat the oil in a large saucepan or stockpot over medium heat and sauté the onion and garlic until the onion is translucent. Add the capsicum, mustard seeds, mustard powder, turmeric, cayenne pepper, ground spice and salt. Cook for about 3 mins.

Add the shredded cabbage and the corn kernels. Give everything a good stir to get the flavours to mingle. Now add the white wine vinegar, sugar and water. Cook, uncovered, for about 20 mins.

Take out a quarter of the hot mixture, allow to cool a little, and, taking care not to scald yourself, blend it roughly, either in a food processor or using a hand-held blender. Return the blended portion to the pot and continue to cook for another 10 mins, until the relish thickens. Keep in an airtight container or clean jar in the fridge for 1–2 months.

If you want to preserve it to store in the pantry, pack into warm sterilised jars (see page 181) and heat-process (see page 180) for 15 mins. Store in the pantry for up to 12 months.

Easy Chilli Vinegar

Splash this vinegar into stir-fries, use as the base of a salad dressing with a kick or drizzle on sliced tomatoes.

Bruise a few chillies, pop them in a jar and cover with salt and the vinegar of your choice. Add the aromatics of your choice, if using. Leave at room temperature to infuse for a few weeks. Strain into a clean and dry airtight bottle and it will basically keep forever.

PREPARATION TIME:
10 mins

STORAGE: **up to 1 year in the pantry or fridge**

MAKES: **1 x 200 ml (7 fl oz/ 1 cup) jar**

4–5 chillies

1 tsp salt

200 ml (7 fl oz/generous ¾ cup) apple cider or white wine vinegar

1 tsp peppercorns, a few bay leaves or a few slices of ginger (optional)

TIP: Add 5–10 drops to lemon honey tea for winter colds and chills.

Chilli Jam

PREPARATION TIME:
30 mins, plus 20 mins sterilising

COOKING TIME: **1½ hours**

STORAGE: **up to 1 year**

MAKES: **4 x 300 ml (10½ fl oz/1¼ cup) jars**

---

100 ml (3½ fl oz/scant ½ cup) vegetable oil

500 g (1 lb 2 oz) onions, thinly sliced

1 tsp ground coriander

1 tsp ground cumin

1 kg (2 lb 4 oz) long red chillies, thinly sliced

500 ml (17 fl oz/2 cups) white wine vinegar

500 ml (17 fl oz/2 cups) water

750 g (1 lb 10 oz) caster (superfine) sugar

2 tsp salt

This is a sweet, spicy jam that makes a perfect replacement for sweet chilli sauce. Try it in marinades for sticky barbecued chicken wings or pork ribs, or with ricotta and salami in a sandwich. We use long red chillies and keep the seeds in, as they generally have plenty of heat without being too fiery, but this is also great with green chillies.

Pour the vegetable oil into a shallow, wide heavy-based pan over medium heat. Add the onion and sauté for 15 mins until they are soft and sweet but not coloured. Stir in the coriander, cumin and chilli, reduce the heat to low and cook for another 15 mins, stirring regularly to prevent the mixture sticking, or until the chilli is very soft. (The chillies and onions need to be very soft to prevent them from becoming candied once the sugar is added.)

Add the vinegar and water, stir well, then cook over medium heat for 10 mins. Add the sugar and salt, stirring to dissolve, then cook for 30–40 mins or until rich, glossy and sticky, stirring occasionally to prevent sticking. Be mindful not to overcook the jam as it will thicken more as it cools.

Meanwhile, sterilise your jars and lids (see page 181).

When your chilli jam has reached setting point, turn off the heat and allow to cool slightly, then carefully fill the hot jars with the hot jam. Remove any air bubbles by gently tapping each jar on the work surface and sliding a butterknife or chopstick around the inside to release any hidden air pockets. Wipe the rims with paper towel or a clean damp cloth and seal. Store in a cool, dark place for up to 12 months.

Roasted Pickled Eggplant

We roast many vegetables before we pickle them, including eggplant (aubergine), red capsicum (pepper), cauliflower, zucchini (courgette) and fennel. The roasting and added oil makes a more antipasto style of pickle, perfect for picnics! For crunchy pickles, you need fresh, crispy vegetables – but for this style, eggplants that are going a little soft will work well.

Preheat the oven to 200°C (400°F). Cut the top and bottom off each eggplant, then cut each eggplant lengthways into quarters. Place on a baking tray, drizzle with the olive oil and sprinkle with 2 teaspoons of the salt. Roast for 20 mins, or until the eggplant is starting to soften and is browning at the edges.

Sterilise your jars and lids (see page 181).

Make your brine by combining the vinegar, water, sugar and 1 teaspoon salt in a non-reactive, medium-sized saucepan. Place over low heat and stir to dissolve the sugar. Increase the heat and allow to simmer for 5 mins.

When the jars are cool enough to handle, put the peppercorns and chilli flakes into each jar.

Strain any excess liquid from the eggplant, then pack each jar half full with eggplant. Add the oregano sprigs and garlic cloves, then pack in the remaining eggplant.

Pour the brine over the eggplant, filling each jar three-quarters of the way. Remove any air bubbles by gently tapping each jar on the work surface and sliding a clean butterknife or chopstick around the inside of the jars to release any hidden air pockets.

Pour in enough oil to cover the eggplant. Wipe the rims of the jars with paper towel or a clean damp cloth and seal immediately.

Leave to cool on the benchtop, then store in the fridge for up to 3 months, or heat-process the jars (see page 180) for 15 mins and store in a cool, dark place for up to 1 year. Once opened, refrigerate and use within 2 months. If the oil solidifies in the fridge, leave the jar at room temperature for an hour before serving.

PREPARATION TIME:
20 mins, plus 20 mins sterilising, plus 15 mins heat-processing (optional)

COOKING TIME: **30 mins**

STORAGE: **up to 3 months in the fridge, or 1 year if heat-processed**

MAKES: **3–4 x 500 ml (17 fl oz/2 cup) jars**

2 kg (4 lb 8 oz) medium-sized eggplants (aubergines)

60 ml (2 fl oz/¼ cup) extra virgin olive oil

1 Tbsp salt

750 ml (26 fl oz/3 cups) white wine vinegar

375 ml (13 fl oz/1½ cups) water

110 g (3¾ oz/½ cup) caster (superfine) sugar

FOR EACH JAR,
YOU WILL NEED:

½ tsp black peppercorns

½ tsp chilli flakes or 1 whole red chilli

2 oregano sprigs

2 garlic cloves, peeled

extra virgin olive oil or vegetable oil, for covering the eggplant

Gherkins

PREPARATION TIME:
20 mins, plus overnight
salting, plus 20 mins
sterilising, plus 15 mins
heat-processing

STORAGE: up to 2 years

MAKES: 2 x 750 ml
(26 fl oz/3 cup) jars

1.2 kg (2 lb 10 oz) small
gherkins (pickling
cucumbers)

1 Tbsp salt

625 ml (21½ fl oz/2½ cups)
white wine vinegar

310 ml (10¾ fl oz/1¼ cups)
water

55–110 g (2–3¾ oz/
¼–½ cup) caster
(superfine) sugar,
depending on how sweet
you like your pickles

2 tsp salt

FOR EACH JAR,
YOU WILL NEED:

¼ tsp whole black
peppercorns

1 tsp dill seeds

¼ tsp dried dill

1 tsp mustard seeds

This is a classic vinegar-based dill pickle. We often get asked where to find gherkins. The only reason you don't see them in supermarkets is that no one buys them raw. If you chat with your greengrocer in early summer, they'll be able to order you a box.

Make sure you don't skip the overnight salting step of this recipe. It makes your pickles stay crunchy and fresh. You can add other flavourings you like to the jars – bay leaves, thyme, lemon peel, peppercorns, caraway and chilli are all delicious. If you're growing dill or fennel at home, let some go to seed, and use the flowers in your jars instead of the dried dill.

Wash the gherkins and remove any blemished ends or flowers that are still attached. If your gherkins are different sizes, cut the big ones in half so they're all similar in size.

Put the gherkins in a non-reactive bowl and sprinkle with the salt. Leave to sit overnight in the fridge. You need to do this in order to draw out excess moisture, or your brine will be too watery. It also helps your pickles keep their crunch.

The next day, strain off and discard any liquid.

Sterilise your jars and lids (see page 181).

Make your brine by combining the vinegar, water, sugar and salt in a non-reactive, medium-sized saucepan. Place over low heat and stir to dissolve the sugar. Increase the heat and bring to the boil.

When the jars are cool enough to handle, add the spices to each jar. Carefully pack the gherkins vertically in the jars. Add the hot brine to completely cover the gherkins. Then add a few more gherkins, laying them horizontally on top to hold the other gherkins down under the brine.

Remove any air bubbles by gently tapping each jar on the work surface and sliding a clean butterknife or chopstick around the inside to release any hidden air pockets. You may need to add more brine to ensure the gherkins are submerged. Wipe the rims of the jars with paper towel or a clean damp cloth and seal.

Heat-process (see page 180) for 15 mins, then let sit for 2 months before opening. Store in a cool, dark place for up to 2 years. Once opened, refrigerate and use within 6 months.

Oven-Dried Preserved Tomatoes

These preserved tomatoes are excellent thinly sliced through pasta, in tomato salads or with ricotta and pepper on toast.

Preheat your oven to its lowest setting. We set ours to 65°C (150°F), but most domestic ovens can only go as low as 100°C (210°F). You can also use a dehydrator if you have one.

Cut your tomatoes in halves or quarters, depending on their size. Lay them on a baking tray lined with baking paper. Sprinkle with the salt and put them in the oven.

For ovens set to 100°C (210°F), the tomatoes can take 7–9 hours to dry. For ovens set to 65°C (150°F), the tomatoes can take 10–12 hours to dry. You want your tomatoes to be mostly dried, but still maintain some plumpness. If your oven feels too hot, you can wedge the door open with a wooden spoon to increase the airflow. (If using a dehydrator, refer to the manufacturer's instructions for advice.) When the tomatoes have finished drying, leave to cool completely.

Sterilise your jars and lids (see page 181).

Make your brine by combining the vinegar, water and sugar in a small, non-reactive saucepan. Place over low heat and stir to dissolve the sugar. Bring to simmering point, then turn off the heat.

When the jars are cool enough to handle, add any flavourings you wish to use, such as 1 garlic clove, 4 peppercorns and 1 thyme sprig. Using small clean tongs or clean hands, carefully pack the dried tomatoes into the jars. Pour the hot brine over the tomatoes, filling each jar only three-quarters of the way up.

Remove any air bubbles by gently tapping each jar on the work surface and sliding a clean butterknife or chopstick around the inside of the jars to release any hidden air pockets. Fill each jar with oil, leaving a 5 mm (¼ inch) gap at the top. Wipe the rims of the jars with paper towel or a clean damp cloth and seal immediately.

Store in a cool, dark place for up to 6 months. Once opened, refrigerate and use within 3 months.

PREPARATION TIME:
20 mins, plus at least 7 hours drying, plus 20 mins sterilising

STORAGE: **up to 6 months**

MAKES: **3 x 300 ml (10½ fl oz/1¼ cup) jars**

2 kg (4 lb 8 oz) tomatoes

2 tsp salt

375 ml (13 fl oz/1½ cups) white wine vinegar

185 ml (6 fl oz/¾ cup) water

75 g (2½ oz/⅓ cup) caster (superfine) sugar

flavourings, such as peeled garlic, black peppercorns, thyme, oregano sprigs, basil stems (optional)

170 ml (5½ fl oz/⅔ cup) olive oil or vegetable oil, or extra to fill jars

Chilli Oil Using Fresh Chillies

PREPARATION TIME:
10 mins, plus 1–2 hours infusing

COOKING TIME: 30 mins

STORAGE: up to 6 months in the fridge

MAKES: 1 x 350 ml (12 fl oz/ scant 1½ cup) jar

375 ml (13 fl oz/ 1½ cups) neutral oil, such as peanut or grapeseed

3 Tbsp Sichuan peppercorns

4 star anise

1 cinnamon stick

10 chillies, chopped

When she's at a Chinese restaurant, our resident fermenter Jaimee Edwards always sits next to the chilli oil, as it's by far her favourite dining companion. Motivated to know how to make her own using the abundance of chillies she grows, she applied the method used to make chilli oil from dried chillies to her fresh ones. The experiment worked, and this fiery oil can be used as a base for a dipping sauce or to cook with as you would any oil.

Pour the oil into a medium saucepan and add the peppercorns, star anise and cinnamon stick. Very slowly heat the oil over low heat for 30 mins. You want to pay close attention to the spices to ensure they're becoming gently aromatic and not burnt – you can soon smell the difference.

Put the chilli in a heatproof bowl or another saucepan and very carefully (we mean super-carefully) pour the hot oil over the chopped chilli. Allow to infuse and cool for 1–2 hours before straining into a clean and dry airtight jar. Keep for up to 6 months in the fridge.

Tomato Ketchup

When Patrice joined the Cornersmith family, he gave us this recipe for tomato ketchup, and it immediately replaced the more time-consuming one we'd been using before. This ketchup is easy for the kids to help make, as well as being sweet and salty enough for them to never go back to the store-bought version. Add cayenne pepper, chilli or smoky paprika to spice things up.

Heat the vegetable oil in a large non-reactive saucepan over medium heat and sauté the onions for about 5 mins until they soften.

Add all the remaining ingredients except the sugar, then reduce the heat to low and simmer for 2 hours, stirring occasionally. Add the sugar and simmer for another 30 mins.

Remove from the heat and blitz with a stick blender. (If you want a very smooth consistency, pass the ketchup through a sieve, pressing down to extract as much liquid – and flavour – as possible.)

Place the pan of ketchup back on the stovetop over low heat, cover with a lid and simmer for 30 mins.

Meanwhile, sterilise your bottles (see page 181). When the bottles are cool enough to handle, pour the hot ketchup into the hot bottles and seal immediately. Heat-process (see page 180) for 10 mins, then store in a cool, dark place for up to 2 years. Once opened, refrigerate and use within 12 months.

PREPARATION TIME:
40 mins, plus 20 mins sterilising, plus 10 mins heat-processing

COOKING TIME: **3 hours**

STORAGE: **up to 2 years**

MAKES: **6 x 250 ml (9 fl oz/ 1 cup) bottles**

60 ml (2 fl oz/¼ cup) vegetable oil

3 large onions, roughly chopped

2.8 kg (6 lb 4 oz) tomatoes, roughly chopped

2 large Granny Smith apples, peeled and cubed

750 ml (26 fl oz/3 cups) white wine vinegar

80 g (2¾ oz/¼ cup) salt

1½ Tbsp ground cloves

1½ Tbsp ground ginger

1½ Tbsp ground coriander

280 g (10 oz/1¼ cups) brown sugar

Red Pepper Relish

PREPARATION TIME:
30 mins, plus 10 mins
heat-processing (optional)

COOKING TIME: about
1¼ hours

STORAGE: up to 6 months,
or up to 2 years if heat-
processed

MAKES: 4 x 300 ml
(10½ fl oz/1¼ cup) jars

170 ml (5½ fl oz/⅔ cup)
olive or vegetable oil

500 g (1 lb 2 oz) onions,
thinly sliced

1.5 kg (3 lb 5 oz) red
capsicum (pepper), cut
into long strips 1–2 cm
(½ inch) thick

2–3 garlic cloves, crushed
or finely chopped

1–2 tsp smoked paprika

2 tsp ground cumin

1 tsp ground caraway
seeds

½ tsp chilli flakes

500 ml (17 fl oz/2 cups) red
wine vinegar

110 g (3¾ oz/½ cup) caster
(superfine) sugar

2 tsp salt

We can't make enough of this relish to keep our customers happy, so here's the recipe. It's great at barbecues or with potatoes and polenta.

Heat the oil in a non-reactive saucepan over medium heat. Add half the onion and sauté for about 10 mins, or until starting to soften. Add the remaining onion and sauté for another 5 mins or so.

Add half the capsicum and cook out any liquid that is released, then add the remaining capsicum and turn up the heat. Stir constantly to soften the vegetables, making sure the excess liquid evaporates and the vegetables aren't stewing in their own juices. This will take around 15–20 mins.

Once the capsicum is soft but not falling apart, add the garlic and sauté until fragrant. Add the spices and mix well.

Now add the vinegar, sugar and salt, stirring until the sugar and salt have dissolved. Turn the heat down to low and cook gently for about 45 mins, or until the relish is starting to thicken. Turn up the heat for the last 5 mins and cook out any excess liquid.

Meanwhile, sterilise your jars and lids (see page 181).

Carefully fill the hot jars with the hot relish. Remove any air bubbles by gently tapping each jar on the work surface and sliding a clean butterknife around the inside to release any hidden air pockets. Wipe the rims of the jars with paper towel or a clean damp cloth and seal immediately.

To extend the shelf life to 2 years, heat-process the jars (see page 180) for 10 mins.

Leave to sit for at least 1 month before eating. Once opened, refrigerate and use within 6 months.

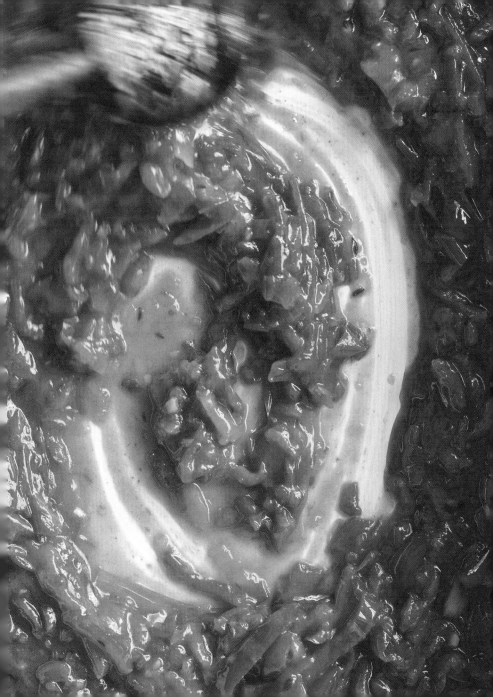

Pickled Watermelon Rind

This is a great recipe to use up the rind from all the watermelon that gets eaten over summer. We toss this pickle through a watermelon and feta salad, but it is also delicious on a cheese plate, or added to other salads.

You can heat-process this pickle to make it last longer, but the texture will be better if you store it in the fridge.

Peel off and discard the green outer skin from the watermelon rind.

Slice the white flesh of the watermelon rind into strips and place in a clean non-reactive container. Sprinkle all over with the salt and leave to stand overnight.

The next day, make your brine by combining the remaining ingredients in a non-reactive, medium-sized saucepan. Place over low heat and stir to dissolve the sugar. Bring to a simmer, then turn off the heat and let the flavours infuse the vinegar for 10 mins or so.

Rinse the salt off your watermelon rind strips and dry with clean paper towel. Place in a clean container. Cover with the hot spicy brine and allow to cool.

Once cool, cover with a lid and store in the fridge. Use within 2 months.

PREPARATION TIME:
20 mins, plus overnight salting

STORAGE: **up to 2 months in the fridge**

MAKES: **1 x 750 ml (26 fl oz/3 cup) jar or container**

250 g (9 oz) peeled watermelon rind

3 Tbsp salt

400 ml (14 fl oz/generous 1½ cups) apple cider vinegar

200 ml (7 fl oz/scant 1 cup) water

165 g (5¾ oz/¾ cup) caster (superfine) sugar

1 tsp salt

4 slices of fresh ginger

½ tsp chilli flakes

1 tsp dried allspice berries

3–4 juniper berries

2 star anise

1 tsp black peppercorns

Sweet Pickled
Stone Fruits

PREPARATION TIME:
**20 mins, plus 20 mins
sterilising, plus 15 mins
heat-processing**

STORAGE: **up to 1 year**

MAKES: **3–4 x 500 ml
(17 fl oz/2 cup) jars**

**600 ml (21 fl oz/2½ cups)
apple cider vinegar**

**300 ml (10½ fl oz/1¼ cups)
water**

**250 g (9 oz/generous
1 cup) white (granulated)
or raw sugar**

**1 kg (2 lb 4 oz) firm stone
fruit of your choice, cut
into quarters or wedges**

FOR EACH JAR,
YOU WILL NEED:

1 cinnamon stick

4 dried allspice berries

1 clove

5 black peppercorns

Pickling is one of our favourite preserving methods for summer fruits. Peaches, nectarines, apricots and plums all work well. Just make sure you use very firm fruit – soft fruit will break down too quickly in the jar.

Experiment with different flavours and combinations: rosemary and peppercorns are great with peaches; ginger and allspice work well with plums.

This brine is sweet and vinegary and makes excellent fruit pickles for a cheese plate, with wintery meats, thinly sliced through a salad, or even served with a dessert. If you're after a more savoury fruit pickle, reduce the sugar by half.

Make your brine by combining the vinegar, water and sugar in a non-reactive, medium-sized saucepan. Place over low heat and stir to dissolve the sugar. Bring to simmering point, then turn off the heat.

Sterilise your jars and lids (see page 181).

When the jars are cool enough to handle, place the spices in the bottom of the jars. Pack the fruit firmly into the hot jars, leaving about 1 cm (½ inch) space at the top.

Bring your brine back up to the boil, then pour the hot brine over the fruit, making sure each piece is completely submerged.

Remove any air bubbles by gently tapping each jar on the work surface and sliding a clean butterknife or chopstick around the inside to release any hidden air pockets. Wipe the rims of the jars with paper towel or a clean damp cloth and seal.

Heat-process the jars (see page 180) for 15 mins, then store in a cool, dark place for up to 1 year. Once opened, refrigerate and use within 6 months.

TIP: Once you've eaten your pickles, save the brine! It's great in cocktails, added to salad dressings or drizzled over cakes.

Pickled Cherries

Sweet pickled cherries are such a treat to have stashed in your pantry. This recipe is nice and easy because you don't even have to pit the cherries!

Try to let these pickles sit for a season or two before you eat them – they get so much better over time, and are amazing with cheese and wine, in cocktails, or sliced through salads.

Once you've eaten all your pickled cherries, don't throw your syrup away! It's great drizzled over fruit with mascarpone, over cakes, or you can reduce it down further and use it as a syrup in soda water or in marinades.

Make your brine by combining the vinegar, water and sugar in a non-reactive, medium-sized saucepan. Place over low heat and stir to dissolve the sugar. Bring to simmering point, then turn off the heat.

Sterilise your jars and lids (see page 181).

When the jars are cool enough to handle, place 4 cloves, 2 star anise and ½ teaspoon peppercorns in the bottom of each jar. Pack the cherries firmly into the hot jars, leaving about 1 cm (½ inch) space at the top.

Bring your brine back up to the boil, then pour the hot brine over the cherries, making sure they are completely submerged. You may need to pack in more cherries once they've softened in the hot brine. The more tightly packed the jars are, the less chance there is of the cherries floating and not preserving properly.

Remove any air bubbles by gently tapping each jar on the work surface and sliding a clean butterknife or chopstick around the inside to release any hidden air pockets. Wipe the rims of the jars with paper towel or a clean damp cloth and seal.

Heat-process the jars (see page 180) for 15 mins, then store in a cool, dark place for up to 18 months. Once opened, refrigerate and use within 6 months.

PREPARATION TIME:
20 mins, plus 20 mins sterilising, plus 15 mins heat-processing

STORAGE: up to 1½ years

MAKES: 2–3 x 500 ml (17 fl oz/2 cup) jars

500 ml (17 fl oz/2 cups) red wine vinegar

250 ml (9 fl oz/1 cup) water

250 g (9 oz/generous 1 cup) raw sugar

8–12 cloves

4–6 star anise

1–1½ tsp black peppercorns

1 kg (2 lb 4 oz) cherries

Tomato Chutney

PREPARATION TIME:
20 mins, plus 1 hour
salting, plus 20 mins
sterilising, plus 15 mins
heat-processing

COOKING TIME: 1½ hours

STORAGE: up to 2 years

MAKES: 4 x 300 ml
(10½ fl oz/1¼ cup) jars

1.5 kg (3 lb 5 oz) ripe red
tomatoes

1 Tbsp salt, plus 1 extra tsp
as needed

80 ml (2½ fl oz/⅓ cup)
olive oil

500g (1 lb 2 oz) onion,
thinly sliced

1 tsp ground turmeric

2 tsp ground coriander

½ Tbsp black mustard
seeds

½ tsp white pepper

100 g (3½ oz) grated
fresh ginger

375 ml (13 fl oz/1½ cups)
white wine vinegar

110 g (3¾ oz/½ cup) caster
(superfine) sugar

A great classic chutney that keeps the taste of summer in your
kitchen all year.

Wash the tomatoes and cut into 2 cm (¾ inch) chunks. Put into a
bowl, sprinkle with salt, mix well and leave to sit for at least an hour
and up to overnight.

Pour the oil into a medium-sized saucepan over medium heat.
Add the onion and sauté until softened and collapsed, but not
browned. Add the spices and ginger and sauté until fragrant.

Drain the excess liquid off the tomato and discard. Add the
tomato chunks to the pan and let simmer until some of the
tomatoey liquid has evaporated and the tomato has thickened
slightly.

Add the vinegar and sugar and mix well.

Cook on medium–low heat for around an hour or so or until the
chutney has thickened. The surface will look rich and glossy and
there will be no puddles of liquid on top. Taste the chutney and add
more salt or white pepper if needed.

Meanwhile, sterilise your jars and lids (see page 181), putting
the jars in the oven about 15 mins before the chutney has finished
cooking.

Fill the hot jars with the hot chutney. Remove any air bubbles
by gently tapping each jar on the work surface and sliding a clean
butterknife around the inside to release any hidden air pockets.
Wipe the rims of the jars with paper towel or a clean damp cloth
and seal immediately.

Heat-process the jars (see page 180) for 15 mins, then store in
a cool, dark place for up to 2 years. Once opened, refrigerate and
use within 3 months.

'What's in the Fruit Bowl' Relish

This is for the fruit bowl dregs at the end of the week, or for those peaches you thought you'd turn into a tart and then promptly forgot about. It's the no-guilt waste hack of your dreams, cleaning out the fruit bowl or the crisper in one hit. Go ahead and use those wrinkly apples, overripe pears, the nectarines that have no flavour, or a combination of everything. Think of it as a fruit-salad relish. This is a recipe for a 1 kg (2 lb 4 oz) batch, but feel free to halve or double the quantities depending on whatever fruit, sugar, vinegar and spices you have on hand. Serve at a barbecue, with cured meats, with bread and cheese, on a burger or with fried eggs.

Heat the oil in a frying pan. Sauté the onion until soft and translucent. Add your chosen flavouring and sauté for another 1–2 mins.

Add the chopped fruit and mix well. Pour in the vinegar, salt and sugar. Simmer gently until the relish is glossy and thick. Some fruits have a lower water content, so if the relish is looking dry but the fruit is still hard, add 60 ml (2 fl oz/¼ cup) water and keep cooking. Taste and adjust the seasoning, adding more spices, seasoning or citrus zest if needed.

Store in a clean jar or airtight container in the fridge for up to 2–3 months. Or spoon into sterilised jars (see page 181), heat-process (see page 180) for 15 mins and store in the pantry for up to 1 year.

PREPARATION TIME: **15 mins**

COOKING TIME: **30 mins**

STORAGE: **2–3 months in the fridge, or up to 1 year if heat-processed**

MAKES: **2 x 250 ml (9 fl oz/ 1 cup) jars**

60 ml (2 fl oz/¼ cup) oil of your choice

1 onion, sliced

1 kg (2 lb 4 oz) chopped fruit (no need to peel)

250 ml (9 fl oz/1 cup) white vinegar, red wine vinegar or apple cider vinegar

1½ tsp salt

110 g (3¾ oz/½ cup) white (granulated) sugar

FLAVOURING OF YOUR CHOICE (CHOOSE 1):

3 Tbsp grated fresh ginger, 2 tsp mustard seeds and ½ tsp ground black pepper

3 sliced garlic cloves, 1–2 sliced chillies, 2 tsp ground cumin and a pinch of cayenne pepper

1 cinnamon stick, 2–3 cloves, the zest of 1 lemon or orange and lots of freshly ground black pepper

PREPARATION TIME:
20 mins

COOKING TIME:
20–30 mins

STORAGE: **up to 3 weeks
in the fridge**

MAKES: **1 x 500 ml (17 fl oz/
2 cup) jar**

**500 g (1 lb 2 oz) wrinkly
vegetables, such as
eggplants (aubergines),
capsicums (peppers),
zucchini (courgettes),
fennel, cauliflower, onions
and chillies**

**3 Tbsp olive or vegetable
oil, plus an extra 80 ml
(2½ fl oz/⅓ cup) to seal
your jar or container**

1 tsp salt

**250 ml (9 fl oz/1 cup) white
wine vinegar**

125 ml (4 fl oz/½ cup) water

**75 g (2½ oz/⅓ cup) caster
(superfine) sugar**

FLAVOURINGS OF YOUR
CHOICE (CHOOSE 2 OR 3):

2 sliced garlic cloves

a little lemon peel or zest

a little orange peel or zest

1 rosemary sprig

1 tsp peppercorns

1 oregano sprig

1 tsp chilli flakes

1 tsp fennel seeds

1 tsp coriander seeds

1 tsp cumin seeds

Roasted Wrinkly Vegetable Pickle

**Make this recipe! This antipasto-style pickle is the most
delicious way to rescue very tired-looking vegetables. By
roasting, then covering the ingredients in a light vinegar brine
and oil, you end up with preserved vegetables, a little like those
you find at Italian delicatessens. This pickle will last for a few
weeks in the fridge if you don't eat it all in one go. We eat it on
toast with ricotta or curd, stirred through pasta or a panzanella
salad, served on a cheese board or pizzas, in burgers and
toasties or as a side at a barbecue. Just don't tell your friends
that it's actually pickled compost!**

Preheat the oven to 180°C (350°F).

Chop your vegetables into good-sized wedges, then place on
a baking tray and drizzle with the olive or vegetable oil and half
the salt. Mix well with your hands to combine, then spread out the
vegetables in an even layer so they have room to char a little at the
edges. Roast for 20–30 mins, until cooked and starting to brown,
but not falling apart.

While your vegetables are roasting, make a brine by combining
the vinegar, water, sugar and remaining salt in a saucepan over low
heat. Stir to dissolve the sugar and salt, then bring to the boil. Once
boiling, remove from the heat.

Place your chosen flavourings in a clean jar or airtight container,
then pack in your roasted vegetables and pour the hot brine over
them, making sure the vegetables are completely covered. Cover
the surface with the extra oil, then seal and store in the fridge for
up to 3 weeks. Allow to sit at least overnight before eating, but it
will taste even better after 3–4 days.

Corn Salsa

The corn season spans the end of summer and the start of autumn, and we often bottle this towards the end of the season. It complements any Mexican-style meal, but is also good with scrambled, poached or fried eggs, or on a chicken or ham sandwich. Try mixing some corn salsa through a bread dough for a simple cornbread or stir a couple of spoonfuls into a firm pancake batter to make quick corn fritters.

Heat the vegetable oil in a large saucepan over medium heat and sauté the onion with the salt until soft. Add the capsicum and sauté for a few mins until starting to soften, then add the corn and sauté for another minute. Mix in the coriander and cayenne, then take off the heat and stir in the green chilli, lime zest and juice.

For the salsa base, combine the vinegar with the water in a non-reactive saucepan. Put the cornflour and turmeric into a heatproof bowl, then stir in 2–3 tablespoons of the vinegar mixture to make a smooth paste. Add the sugar to the vinegar mixture, then place over medium heat and stir until the sugar has dissolved. When the mixture reaches simmering point, transfer it to a jug, then slowly pour into the cornflour paste, whisking as you go until you have a smooth, thick sauce. Leave to cool.

Pour the cooled salsa base over the corn mixture and stir to coat evenly. The salsa can be served straightaway or kept in the fridge for up to 1 month.

If you want to bottle the salsa to store for use later in the year, or to give as a gift, pack it into sterilised jars (see page 181) and heat-process (see page 180) for 10 mins. Unopened jars can be stored in a cool, dark place for up to 12 months; once opened, refrigerate and use within a couple of months.

PREPARATION TIME:
15 mins

COOKING TIME:
30 mins, plus 10 mins heat-processing (optional)

STORAGE: **up to 1 month in the fridge, or 1 year if heat-processed**

MAKES: **about 4 x 300 ml (10½ fl oz/1¼ cup) jars**

1½ Tbsp vegetable oil

1 large onion, finely chopped

1 Tbsp salt

2 small red capsicums (peppers), diced

5 small corncobs, kernels cut from cobs

½ tsp ground coriander

pinch of cayenne

5 green chillies, sliced

finely grated zest and juice of ½ lime

250 ml (9 fl oz/1 cup) white wine vinegar

250 ml (9 fl oz/1 cup) water

2 Tbsp cornflour (cornstarch)

¼ tsp ground turmeric

1½ Tbsp caster (superfine) sugar

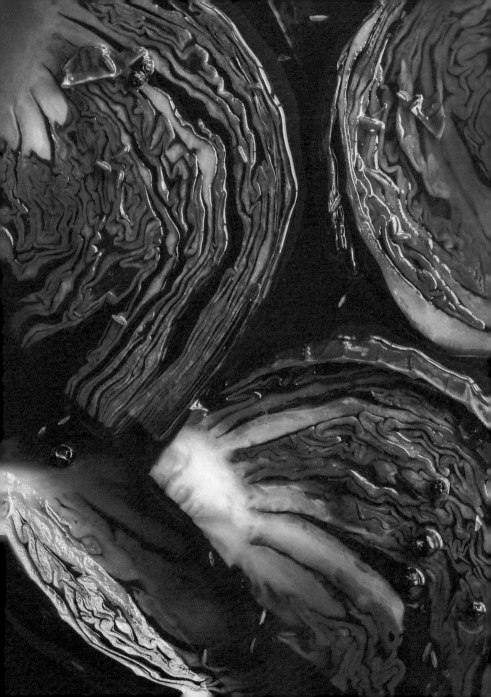

Autumn

IN SEASON: Cabbage, cauliflower, fennel, grapes, lime, mushroom, okra, plum, rhubarb

Pickled Garlicky Mushrooms

PREPARATION TIME:
30 mins, plus 20 mins sterilising

STORAGE: **up to 3 months in the fridge**

MAKES: **2 x 300 ml (10½ fl oz/1¼ cup) jars**

---

250 ml (9 fl oz/1 cup) red wine vinegar

250 ml (9 fl oz/1 cup) water

55 g (2 oz/¼ cup) raw sugar

1 tsp salt

500 g (1 lb 2 oz) Swiss brown or button mushrooms

4 garlic cloves, peeled (see Tip)

1 rosemary sprig, cut in half

2 thyme sprigs

½ tsp black peppercorns

vegetable oil or olive oil, for filling the jars (optional)

All mushrooms work well for pickling. We use Swiss brown, button or chestnut mushrooms, but you could also use pine mushrooms if you're lucky enough to find some. Just remember that pine mushrooms turn a bit gelatinous over time, so rinse them off before serving.

Pickled mushrooms are great in salads, pasta sauces and risotto, and as part of a shared plate.

Make your brine by combining the vinegar, water, sugar and salt in a non-reactive, medium-sized saucepan. Place over low heat and stir to dissolve the sugar. Bring to simmering point, add the mushrooms and simmer in the brine for 2–5 mins, or until softened slightly; be careful not to overcook.

Sterilise your jars and lids (see page 181).

When the jars are cool enough to handle, place 2 garlic cloves, ½ rosemary sprig, 1 thyme sprig and a few peppercorns into the bottom of each jar. Using a slotted spoon or tongs, remove the mushrooms from the brine and carefully but tightly pack them into the jars. Pour the hot brine over, making sure the mushrooms are completely submerged. If you like, you can top the mushrooms with a 1 cm (½ inch) layer of oil.

Remove any air bubbles by gently tapping each jar on the work surface and sliding a clean butterknife or chopstick around the inside to release any hidden air pockets. Wipe the rims of the jars with paper towel or a clean damp cloth and seal.

Store in the fridge for up to 3 months.

TIP: Garlic reacts to vinegar by turning blue. It's still edible but can be a little unsettling to look at. If you wish to avoid this, blanch the garlic cloves for 10 seconds in boiling water before putting them in your jars.

Pickled Red Grapes

It might be more unusual to see fruit instead of vegetables in a pickling liquid, but we pickle lots of fruit and find the vinegar offsets its sweetness beautifully. These pickled grapes go well with soft cheese – try them on top of baked ricotta – and they make an interesting addition to a salad or roasted meat dishes (just add them to the roasting tin about 5 mins before the end of the cooking time). Other fruit that can be successfully pickled include quinces, pears, plums or sugar plums, rhubarb and cumquats.

First sterilise your jars and lids (see page 181).

Make a brine by putting the vinegar, sugar and water in a small non-reactive saucepan over low heat. Stir until the sugar has dissolved, then increase the heat and bring to the boil. Take off the heat.

When the jars are cool enough to handle, put 2 allspice berries, 4 peppercorns and a slice of ginger into each one. Carefully pack in the grapes (see page 179 for packing techniques), then let them soften in the hot brine for a few mins; they will shrink and you may be able to pack in some more. Remove any air bubbles by gently tapping each jar on the work surface and sliding a butterknife or chopstick around the inside to release any hidden air pockets. You may need to add more grapes or brine after doing this (the liquid should reach about 1 cm/½ inch from the top of the jar). Wipe the rims of the jars with paper towel or a clean damp cloth and seal, then heat-process (see page 180) for 15 mins.

Store in a cool, dark place for at least a month before using. Unopened jars will keep for up to 12 months; once opened, refrigerate and use within 3 months.

PREPARATION TIME:
25 mins, plus 15 mins
heat-processing

STORAGE: up to 1 year

MAKES: 3–4 x 400 ml
(14 oz/generous
1½ cup) jars

500 ml (17 fl oz/2 cups) red wine vinegar

440 g (15½ oz/2 cups) caster (superfine) sugar

500 ml (17 fl oz/2 cups) water

4–6 dried allspice berries

8–12 black peppercorns

2–3 slices of fresh ginger

1 kg (2 lb 4 oz) red grapes

Preserved Mushrooms in Oil

PREPARATION TIME:
20 mins

COOKING TIME: 15 mins

STORAGE: up to 2 weeks
in the fridge

MAKES: 1 x 500 ml
(17 fl oz/2 cup) jar

250 ml (9 fl oz/1 cup) white
wine vinegar

2 Tbsp salt

500 ml (17 fl oz/2 cups)
water

500 g (1 lb 2 oz) pine, field,
Swiss brown or chestnut
mushrooms, cleaned and
cut into thick slices

olive oil, to cover

This is based on an Italian style of preserving, where the vegetables are cooked in a vinegar brine, strained and then covered in oil. Treated this way, your mushrooms will keep for a couple of weeks in the fridge. If you like, you can also add some other flavourings. A sprig of rosemary and a few peppercorns in the bottom of each jar is a good combination, or try thyme, bay and lemon zest. Serve these mushrooms as part of an antipasto platter or stir them through sauces – they're especially good with meat.

Combine the vinegar and salt with the water in a non-reactive, medium-sized saucepan. Place over low heat and bring to a simmer, stirring to dissolve the salt.

Working in batches, drop the mushroom slices into the hot brine and simmer for a minute or two until tender. Remove with a slotted spoon and squeeze out the excess liquid, before packing into a clean jar and covering with olive oil. Seal and keep in the fridge for up to 2 weeks.

Kitchen-Scrap Kimchi

Kimchi is one of Korea's great culinary gifts to the world. There are many kimchis, from white kimchi to delicate kimchis made with rice water. For this recipe, use up whatever vegetables you have on hand, but keep in mind that a great kimchi balances salty, sour, spicy and a touch of sweet.

PREPARATION TIME:
45 mins, plus 2–7 days fermenting

STORAGE: up to 6 months in the fridge

MAKES: 3 x 500 ml (17 fl oz/2 cup) jars

500 g (1 lb 2 oz) wombok (Chinese cabbage)

500 g (1 lb 2 oz) daikon

750 g (1 lb 10 oz) mixed vegetables and fruit, such as pumpkin (winter squash), carrots, kale and kale stems, chokos (chayote), nashi pears and radish tops

100 g (3½ oz) fresh ginger

4 garlic cloves, crushed

1 Tbsp chilli flakes

1¼ Tbsp salt

Wash all the vegetables. Tear the wombok into small pieces and place in a large mixing bowl.

Peel the daikon, then grate the daikon and ginger into another bowl. Add the garlic, chilli and salt and mix together. This wet mixture is now your paste.

Prepare whatever other vegetables you are using. Cut them in a uniform way, to the same size.

Add these vegetables to your wombok and gently massage together until all the water is released. Once your vegetables feel wet, add your daikon paste and keep massaging. You want to be able to pick up a handful of vegetables and see water running when you give them a gentle squeeze.

Pack your vegetables into clean jars, pressing down to release air bubbles as you go, and leaving 2 cm (¾ inch) space at the top of the jars. The surface of your vegetables should be covered with 1 cm (½ inch) of liquid. If not, top up with water. Wipe the rim of the jars with paper towel or a clean damp cloth and seal.

Place your jars out of direct sunlight for 2–7 days, depending on the ambient temperature. The warmer the weather, the faster your vegetables will ferment. Open your jar every few days to 'burp' your ferment – this will release the built-up carbon dioxide, and prevent brine spilling out of the jar. Just be sure to press down your kimchi afterwards, so that the brine is covering the top by at least 1 cm (½ inch). If any brine does escape, simply wipe the jar down.

After 2 days, taste your kimchi. If you like it, put it in the refrigerator, where it will last for up to 6 months. If you want to ferment your kimchi further, keep checking and tasting every 2 days until you're happy with the flavour, then store in the fridge.

Pickled Sardines

PREPARATION TIME:
30 mins, plus 1–2 days brining and pickling

STORAGE: **up to 1 month in the fridge**

3 Tbsp salt

1 litre (35 fl oz/4 cups) water

500 g (1 lb 2 oz) butterflied sardines (about 8 small ones)

1 red onion, thinly sliced

1 lemon, thinly sliced

PICKLING LIQUID

500 ml (17 fl oz/2 cups) white wine vinegar

55 g (2 oz/¼ cup) caster (superfine) sugar

1 tsp mustard seeds

2 tsp dried allspice berries

2 tsp black peppercorns

1 tsp dill seeds

3 bay leaves

3 cloves

250 ml (9 fl oz/1 cup) water

Thanks to Cornersmith head chef Sabine's European background, we served lots of pickled and smoked fish. First the fish is steeped in brine to break it down, then it's pickled to preserve it. Oily fish such as herring and sardines really benefit from this treatment, as the vinegar in the pickling liquid helps to cut through the richness of the fish. These sardines can be served on toast or with a salad. If you get a taste for them, it's worth making a bigger quantity, as they'll keep for up to a month in the fridge; just pack the brined sardines in layers with the onion, lemon and spices in sterilised jars (see page 181). Both the brine and the pickling liquid can be made ahead of time.

Put the salt and water in a non-reactive saucepan and heat just enough to dissolve the salt. Leave to cool completely, then immerse the sardines in this brine and refrigerate for at least 8 hours, or up to 24 hours.

For the pickling liquid, put all the ingredients into a non-reactive saucepan. Bring to the boil, stirring every now and then so the sugar dissolves evenly. Let it bubble for 2 mins, then remove from the heat and leave to cool completely.

Take the sardines out of the brine and pat dry with paper towel. Place the sardines in a clean non-reactive container, layering them with the onion and lemon slices. Pour the pickling liquid over the sardines, then refrigerate for at least a day before using. Drain before serving.

Pickled Celery with Lemon & Peppercorns

This recipe is a good one when you've got half a bunch of celery left over. We store these pickles in the fridge to keep them crisp and crunchy. Try thinly slicing them and tossing them through tabouleh or other grainy salads. Pickled celery is also amazing in a bloody mary!

PREPARATION TIME:
20 mins, plus 20 mins
sterilising, plus 10 mins
heat-processing

STORAGE: up to 3 months
in the fridge, or 6 months
if heat-processed

MAKES: 2 x 300 ml
(10½ fl oz/1¼ cup) jars

3–4 celery stalks (see Tip)

250 ml (9 fl oz/1 cup) white wine vinegar

250 ml (9 fl oz/1 cup) water

55 g (2 oz/¼ cup) caster (superfine) sugar

1 tsp salt

FOR EACH JAR,
YOU WILL NEED:

1 strip of lemon peel

1 bay leaf

3 black peppercorns

¼ tsp dill seeds

¼ tsp celery seeds (optional)

Wash the celery well and cut into strips or 5 cm (2 inch) chunks.

Sterilise your jars and lids (see page 181).

Make your brine by combining the vinegar, water, sugar and salt in a non-reactive, medium-sized saucepan. Place over low heat and stir to dissolve the sugar. Bring to the boil, then turn off the heat.

When the jars are cool enough to handle, put the lemon peel strip, bay leaf and peppercorns in the bottom of each jar. Add the dill and celery seeds, then carefully but tightly pack in the celery.

Cover with the hot brine, making sure the celery is completely submerged.

Remove any air bubbles by gently tapping each jar on the work surface and sliding a clean butterknife or chopstick around the inside to release any hidden air pockets. Wipe the rims of the jars with paper towel or a clean damp cloth and seal immediately.

We prefer to keep these pickles in the fridge as the cold helps them keep their crunch; they will keep in the fridge for 3 months. To extend the shelf life to 6 months, heat-process the jars (see page 180) for 10 mins, then store in a cool, dark place. Once opened, refrigerate and use within 3 months.

TIP: Save the leaves from the celery and use them in salads.

Gari (Japanese-Style Pickled Ginger)

This tastes exactly like sushi-train ginger, only better! The ginger reacts to the vinegar and salt and turns a very pretty pink. Use this pickle thinly sliced through noodle salads, in dipping sauces or with sushi or fish.

There is no need to peel the ginger – just give it a good wash. Slice the ginger as finely as you can, using a mandoline or a very sharp knife. Put the ginger slices in a bowl and cover with the salt, mixing it through with your hands. Leave to stand for 1–2 hours.

Sterilise your jars and lids (see page 181).

Strain any excess water from the ginger slices and discard. Lay the slices on a clean paper towel or tea towel (dish towel) and press out any excess salt and moisture.

Make your brine by combining the vinegar and sugar in a small non-reactive saucepan over low heat. Stir to dissolve the sugar and bring to simmering point.

When the jars are cool enough to handle, carefully pack the ginger into the warm jars.

Pour the hot brine over the ginger slices, making sure they are completely submerged.

Remove any air bubbles by gently tapping each jar on the work surface and sliding a clean butterknife or chopstick around the inside to release any hidden air pockets. Wipe the rims of the jars with paper towel or a clean damp cloth and seal immediately.

Leave to cool on the benchtop, then store in a cool, dark place for up to 3 months, or in the fridge for up to 6 months. Once opened, refrigerate and use within 6 months.

PREPARATION TIME: 25 mins, plus 1–2 hours salting, plus 20 mins sterilising

STORAGE: up to 3 months in the pantry, or 6 months in the fridge

MAKES: 3–4 x 200 ml (7 fl oz/scant 1 cup) jars

400 g (14 oz) fresh ginger

2 Tbsp salt

500 ml (17 fl oz/2 cups) rice wine vinegar, with an acidity of at least 5%

110 g (3¾ oz/½ cup) caster (superfine) sugar

Chilli-Pickled Okra

This hot pickled okra is delicious and adds a real punch of flavour and heat to any Mexican-style dishes. Serve it with tortillas and beans, or thinly sliced through slaws.

Many people don't like the 'sliminess' of okra, which is due to its high mucilage content. If you keep the okra whole and are careful not to pierce or break the skin, the gooey mucilage will not leach out.

Sterilise your jars and lids (see page 181).

Make your brine by combining the vinegar, water, sugar, salt and cayenne pepper in a non-reactive, medium-sized saucepan. Place over low heat and stir to dissolve the sugar and salt. Bring to simmering point, then turn off the heat.

When the jars are cool enough to handle, put the garlic, ginger, coriander seeds and peppercorns into the bottom of each jar.

Using small clean tongs or clean hands, carefully but tightly pack the raw whole okra in, packing them vertically, with some stems facing up and some stems facing down. Pour in the hot brine, making sure all the okra is completely submerged.

Remove any air bubbles by gently tapping each jar on the work surface and sliding a clean butterknife or chopstick around the inside to release any hidden air pockets. Wipe the rims of the jars with paper towel or a clean damp cloth and seal immediately.

Leave to cool on the benchtop, then store in the fridge for up to 3 months, or heat-process the jars for 10 mins and store in a cool, dark place for up to 1 year.

Allow to sit for at least 2 weeks before eating. Once opened, refrigerate and use within 6 months.

PREPARATION TIME:
10 mins, plus 20 mins sterilising, plus 10 mins heat-processing (optional)

STORAGE: up to 3 months in the fridge, or 1 year if heat-processed

MAKES: 2 x 500 ml (17 fl oz/2 cup) jars

500 ml (17 fl oz/2 cups) white wine vinegar

250 ml (9 fl oz/1 cup) water

55 g (2 oz/¼ cup) caster (superfine) sugar

2 tsp salt

pinch of cayenne pepper

500 g (1 lb 2 oz) okra, washed

FOR EACH JAR,
YOU WILL NEED:

1 garlic clove, peeled

2 slices fresh ginger

¼ tsp coriander seeds

¼ tsp black peppercorns

1 tsp chilli flakes or 1 whole small chilli

Knotted Snake Bean Pickles

PREPARATION TIME:
20 mins

STORAGE: **up to 3 months in the fridge**

MAKES: **1 x 750 ml (26 fl oz) jar**

1 big bunch of snake (long) beans, about 300–400 g (10½–14 oz)

500 ml (17 fl oz/2 cups) white wine vinegar

250 ml (9 fl oz/1 cup) water

75 g (2½ oz/⅓ cup) caster (superfine) sugar

2 tsp salt

¼ tsp ground turmeric

½ tsp black peppercorns

1 tsp dill seeds

2 garlic cloves, peeled

1 tsp chilli flakes (optional)

Green beans make great pickles! And these knotted snake (long) bean pickles are delicious and adorable. They are best kept in the fridge, as snake beans tend to get a bit slimy over time.

Wash the beans and trim off any blemished ends. Tie any long beans into loose knots or coils.

Make your brine by combining the vinegar, water, sugar, salt and turmeric in a non-reactive, medium-sized saucepan. Place over low heat and stir to dissolve the sugar and salt. Bring to simmering point, add your knotted beans and blanch for 2–3 mins, then turn off the heat.

Put the peppercorns and dill seeds in the bottom of a clean jar. Add the garlic and chilli flakes, if using, then carefully pack the beans in. Add the hot brine (see Tip), making sure the beans are completely submerged.

Remove any air bubbles by gently tapping the jar on the work surface and sliding a clean butterknife or chopstick around the inside to release any hidden air pockets. Wipe the rim of the jar with paper towel or a clean damp cloth and seal immediately. The beans will keep in the fridge for up to 3 months.

TIP: Any leftover brine can be stored in the fridge for up to 1 month and used for pickling and quick-pickling, or as a base for salad dressings.

Lime Pickle

Lime pickle is one of our favourite autumn preserves. This pickle is wonderful with curries, seafood and fried eggs. You can also mix a tablespoon through yoghurt to make a flavoursome marinade for chicken or fish.

Put the limes in a saucepan with the water. Simmer over medium heat for 20–30 mins until soft.

Strain the limes, then leave to cool slightly. Cut the limes into very thin strips, or finely dice them. Set aside in a bowl, making sure you add all the lime pulp.

Heat the vegetable oil in a large non-reactive saucepan. Sauté the onion over medium heat for about 8 mins, until soft, translucent and sweet. Add the garlic and sauté for 1–2 mins until fragrant.

Turn the heat down to low. Add the lime, vinegar, sugar, salt, spices and curry leaves, stirring to combine. Simmer for 15 mins, or until the sauce thickens, stirring often so it doesn't stick to the pan. Don't let it dry out too much, as you need moisture to cover the limes once they're packed into the jars.

Meanwhile, sterilise your jars and lids (see page 181).

Carefully fill the hot jars with the hot pickle. Remove any air bubbles by gently tapping each jar on the work surface and sliding a clean butterknife or chopstick around the inside to release any hidden air pockets. Wipe the rims of the jars with paper towel or a clean damp cloth and seal immediately.

Leave to cool on the benchtop, then store in a cool, dark place for up to 6 months. To extend the shelf life to 2 years, heat-process the jars (see page 180) for 10 mins. Let the lime pickle sit for at least 2 months before eating; it will be even better after 6 months. Once opened, refrigerate and use within 6 months.

TIP: To toast the spice seeds, gently fry them in a small frying pan without any oil for a minute or two until aromatic, stirring constantly so they don't burn. It's best to toast them separately, as fenugreek seeds need only a very quick fry to avoid bitterness. Grind to a powder using a spice grinder or mortar and pestle.

PREPARATION TIME:
40 mins, plus 20 mins sterilising, plus 10 mins heat-processing (optional)

COOKING TIME:
about 1 hour

STORAGE: **6 months, or up to 2 years if heat-processed**

MAKES: **3–4 x 300 ml (10½ fl oz/1¼ cup) jars**

1 kg (2 lb 4 oz) limes (preferably unwaxed)

3 litres (105 fl oz/12 cups) water

80 ml (2½ fl oz/⅓ cup) vegetable oil

500 g (1 lb 2 oz) onions, thinly sliced

3–4 garlic cloves, crushed

375 ml (13 fl oz/1½ cups) white wine vinegar

110 g (3¾ oz/½ cup) caster (superfine) sugar

1 Tbsp salt

1 tsp fenugreek seeds, toasted and ground (see Tip)

2 tsp cumin seeds, toasted and ground (see Tip)

2 tsp coriander seeds, toasted and ground (see Tip)

1–2 tsp chilli flakes

½ tsp ground turmeric

6–8 curry leaves

Plum & Ginger Chutney

PREPARATION TIME:
45 mins, plus 20 mins sterilising, plus 10 mins heat-processing

COOKING TIME: **1¼ hours**

STORAGE: **up to 2 years**

MAKES: **4 x 300 ml (10½ fl oz) jars**

1.5 kg (3 lb 5 oz) plums

80 ml (2½ fl oz/⅓ cup) vegetable oil

500 g (1 lb 2 oz) onion, thinly sliced

60 g (2¼ oz/⅓ cup) grated fresh ginger

1 tsp brown or yellow mustard seeds

½ tsp chilli flakes

¼ tsp ground cloves, or 3 whole cloves

½ tsp ground cinnamon

½ tsp freshly ground black pepper

250 ml (9 fl oz/1 cup) white wine vinegar

110 g (3¾ oz/½ cup) raw sugar

2 tsp salt

This chutney is good to make at the end of plum season, when there's an abundance of cheap, delicious plums. We also use this recipe for summer stone fruits – peaches, nectarines and apricots. You can use apple cider vinegar or red wine vinegar if you prefer; just remember your vinegars need to be 5 per cent acidity or more for preserving.

Cut the plums into 2 cm (¾ inch) cubes and discard the stones.

Heat the vegetable oil in a large non-reactive saucepan and sauté the onion over medium heat for about 8 mins, until soft and collapsed. Add the ginger and spices and stir for another minute or two until fragrant. Add the plum and stir until the onion, plum and spices are evenly mixed. Add the vinegar, sugar and salt, stirring until the sugar and salt have dissolved.

Reduce the heat to low, stirring regularly to make sure the chutney isn't sticking. Cook for about 1 hour, until the desired consistency is reached. The chutney should be glossy and thick, with no puddles of liquid on top. Taste halfway through and add more spices or salt if needed; if your plums are very tart, you can add an extra 3 tablespoons or so of raw or brown sugar.

Sterilise your jars and lids (see page 181), putting the jars in the oven about 15 mins before the chutney has finished cooking.

Carefully ladle the hot chutney into the hot jars.

Remove any air bubbles by gently tapping each jar on the work surface and sliding a clean butterknife or chopstick around the inside to release any hidden air pockets. Wipe the rims of the jars with paper towel or a clean damp cloth and seal immediately.

Heat-process the jars (see page 180) for 10 mins, then store in a cool, dark place for up to 2 years.

Leave to sit for 2–3 months before eating; this chutney gets better and better with time. Once opened, refrigerate and use within 6 months.

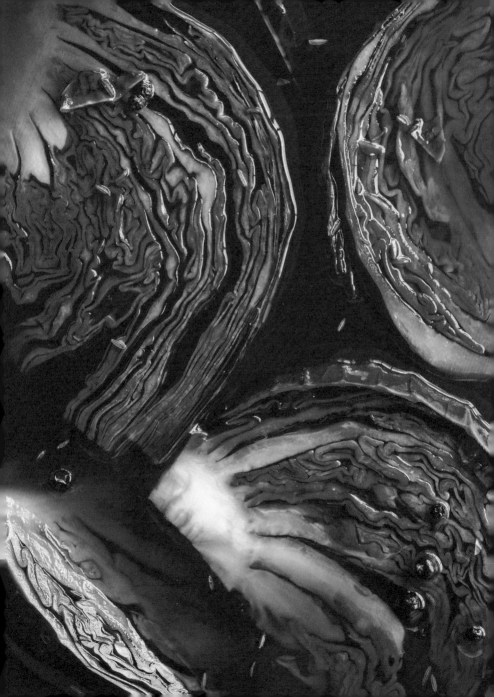

Quick Pickled Cabbage Wedges

Here's the perfect pickle when you've bought a whole cabbage for a slaw and end up having some left over in the bottom of your fridge. It's super easy to prepare, full of flavour, and makes midweek sausages and mash even more delicious. Serve it sliced with pulled pork, or thinly sliced and tossed through salads for extra tang.

Slice the cabbage into large 5 cm (2 inch) wedges.

Make your brine by combining the vinegar, water, sugar and salt in a non-reactive, medium-sized saucepan. Place over low heat and stir to dissolve the sugar. Add the spices and bring to the boil.

Put your cabbage wedges in a heatproof glass container and cover with the hot brine.

Allow to cool, then seal and store in the fridge for up to 1 month. It will take about 3–4 days for the wedges to be pickled.

PREPARATION TIME:
20 mins

STORAGE: **up to 1 month in the fridge**

MAKES: **1 x 1 litre (35 fl oz/ ¼ cup) container**

½ small red cabbage, cut into wedges

500 ml (17 fl oz/2 cups) red wine vinegar

375 ml (13 fl oz/1½ cups) water

110 g (3¾ oz/½ cup) caster (superfine) sugar

2 tsp salt

1 tsp caraway seeds

1 tsp black peppercorns

½ tsp juniper berries

Tumeric-Pickled Cauliflower Stems

PREPARATION TIME:
15 mins

STORAGE: **up to 2–3 weeks in the fridge**

MAKES: **1 x 300 ml (10½ fl oz/1¼ cup) jar**

1 cauliflower stem (80–100 g)

125 ml (4 fl oz/½ cup) white wine vinegar

125 ml (4 fl oz/½ cup) water

2 Tbsp raw sugar

½ tsp salt

½ tsp caraway seeds

½ tsp black peppercorns

a small pinch of ground turmeric

a small pinch of chilli flakes

Instead of throwing cauliflower stems in the bin, pickle them! Serve with falafel, garlic dip and flatbread, stirred through a grain salad or in a sandwich.

Thinly slice the cauliflower and put it into a clean jar or container.

Heat the vinegar, water, raw sugar, salt, caraway seeds, peppercorns, turmeric and chilli flakes in a small non-reactive saucepan over medium heat. Stir to dissolve the sugar and bring to the boil, then pour over the cauliflower. Seal the jar immediately.

Allow to sit in the fridge for a few days before eating; it should last for 2–3 weeks in the fridge.

Cauliflower Relish

PREPARATION TIME:
20 mins

COOKING TIME: 45 mins

STORAGE: 1–2 months in
the fridge, or up to 1 year
if heat-processed

MAKES: 3–4 x 300 ml
(10½ fl oz/1¼ cup) jars

2 Tbsp neutral oil

1 onion, diced

3 garlic cloves, diced

1 leek or celery stalk, diced

3 tsp mustard seeds

2 Tbsp mustard powder

a good pinch of turmeric

¼ tsp cayenne pepper

1 tsp of your favourite
ground spice (cumin,
allspice, ginger)

2 tsp salt

75 g (2½ oz/1 cup)
shredded cabbage

650 g (1 lb 7 oz)
cauliflower, chopped

375 ml (13 fl oz/1½ cups)
white wine vinegar

110 g (3¾ oz/½ cup) white
(granulated) sugar

125 ml (4 fl oz/½ cup) water

If you've got half a cauliflower left in the fridge at the end of the week and are looking for something delicious to do with it, try this relish. Tangy and moreish, this will be amazing on toasties, in salad sandwiches and with cheese and crackers in the weeks to come.

Heat the oil in a large saucepan or stockpot over medium heat and sauté the onion and garlic until the onion is translucent. Add the leek or celery, mustard seeds, mustard powder, turmeric, cayenne pepper, ground spice and salt. Cook for about 3 mins.

Add the shredded cabbage and the cauliflower. Give everything a good stir to get the flavours to mingle. Now add the white wine vinegar, sugar and water. Cook, uncovered, for about 20 mins.

Take out a quarter of the hot mixture, allow to cool a little, and, taking care not to scald yourself, blend it roughly, either in a food processor or using a hand-held blender. Return the blended portion to the pot and continue to cook for another 10 mins, until the relish thickens. Keep in an airtight container or clean jar in the fridge for 1–2 months.

If you want to preserve it to store in the pantry, pack into warm sterilised jars (see page 181) and heat-process (see page 180) for 15 mins. Store in the pantry for up to 12 months.

Pickled Sprouts for the Very Brave

We've pickled some very odd things over the years, and pickled Brussels sprouts made us laugh out loud, but they're surprisingly delicious, especially with lots of caraway seeds, peppercorns and garlic cloves in the jar. Go on, give them a go.

Sterilise your jars and lids (see page 181).

Prepare the Brussels sprouts by giving them a quick blanch in salted boiling water.

Make the pickling liquid by combining the vinegar, water, sugar and salt in a non-reactive, medium-sized saucepan over medium heat. Stir to dissolve the sugar and salt. Increase the heat, bring to simmering point, then remove from the heat. Put up to 1 tablespoon of the whole spices and 2 garlic cloves in each jar.

Pack the sprouts into the sterilised jars using small clean tongs or clean hands. Cover with brine until the vegetables are completely submerged. Remove any air bubbles by gently tapping each jar on the work surface and sliding a butterknife or chopstick around the inside to release any hidden air pockets. Wipe the rim of the jar with paper towel or a clean damp cloth and seal.

Store in the fridge for up to 3 months, or heat-process (see page 180) for 15 mins and store in the pantry for up to 1 year. These pickles get better over time, so let them sit for at least a few weeks before eating.

PREPARATION TIME: 20 mins, plus 20 mins sterilising

STORAGE: 3 months in the fridge, or up to 1 year if heat-processed

MAKES: 4 × 400 ml (14 oz/ generous 1½ cup) jars

1 kg (2 lb 4 oz) Brussels sprouts

500 ml (17 fl oz/2 cups) apple cider or white wine vinegar

250 ml (9 fl oz/1 cup) water

110 g (3¾ oz/½ cup) white (granulated) sugar

at least 2 tsp salt

4 Tbsp whole spices, such as caraway seeds amd peppercorns

8 garlic cloves

Rhubarb & Red Onion Relish

PREPARATION TIME:
30 mins, plus 20 mins
sterilising, plus 10 mins
heat-processing (optional)

COOKING TIME: about
1 hour

STORAGE: 6 months in the
fridge, or up to 2 years if
heat-processed

MAKES: 4 x 300 ml
(10½ fl oz/1¼ cup) jars

1 kg (2 lb 4 oz) rhubarb stalks,
washed, trimmed and cut
into 5 cm (2 inch) lengths

2 Tbsp caster (superfine)
sugar

500 ml (17 fl oz/2 cups) red
wine vinegar

80 ml (2½ fl oz/⅓ cup)
vegetable oil

500 g (1 lb 2 oz) red onion,
thinly sliced

50 g (1¾ oz) grated
fresh ginger

1 tsp ground cumin

1 tsp ground coriander

½ tsp ground fenugreek

2–3 garlic cloves, crushed

500 g (1 lb 2 oz) apples,
peeled and grated

200 g (7 oz/1 scant cup)
brown sugar

1–2 tsp salt

Lovely with cheddar, eggs or at a barbecue or Christmas lunch, this is an excellent relish to stock in the pantry or give as a gift. Roasting the rhubarb really intensifies the flavour, so don't skip this step. It also cuts down on cooking time, once it's in the pot.

Preheat the oven to 180°C (350°F). Spread the rhubarb evenly over two baking trays. Sprinkle with the caster sugar and 80 ml (2½ fl oz/⅓ cup) of the vinegar. Mix with your hands to combine. Roast the rhubarb for about 20 mins until soft and slightly caramelised.

Meanwhile, heat the vegetable oil in a non-reactive, medium-sized saucepan. Add the onion and sauté over medium heat for about 8 mins, until soft and translucent. Add the ginger, spices and garlic and sauté for 2 mins until fragrant, stirring constantly.

Add the roasted rhubarb to the pan, along with the remaining vinegar, grated apple, brown sugar and salt, stirring to combine well. Reduce the heat to low.

Simmer, uncovered, for about 30 mins, stirring now and then, until the relish is thick and glossy, with no puddles on the surface.

Meanwhile, sterilise your jars and lids (see page 181).

Carefully fill the hot jars with the hot relish. Remove any air bubbles by gently tapping each jar on the work surface and sliding a clean butterknife or chopstick around the inside to release any hidden air pockets. Wipe the rims of the jars with paper towel or a clean damp cloth and seal immediately.

Leave to cool on the benchtop, then store in the fridge for up to 6 months. To extend the shelf life to 2 years, heat-process the jars (see page 180) for 10 mins.

Once opened, refrigerate and use within 3 months.

TIP: If you have some relish left over after you've filled your jars, store it in an airtight container in the fridge and use within 3 weeks.

Pickled Rhubarb

This sweet pickle is delicious on a cheese plate, with cold meats, or thinly sliced through salads; you could also use this brine for pickling plums, cherries or other red fruits. Once you've eaten all of your pickles, save the brine to make a full-flavoured syrup that's great in cocktails, dressings, marinades and not-so-sweet desserts.

PREPARATION TIME: 20 mins, plus 20 mins sterilising

STORAGE: 2–3 months, or up to 6 months if heat-processed

MAKES: 2–3 x 500 ml (17 fl oz/2 cup) jars

Sterilise your jars and lids (see page 181).

Meanwhile, trim the rhubarb stalks, making sure there are no green leaves attached. Cut the stalks into lengths to fit the jars.

Make your brine by combining the vinegar, sugar, water and honey in a non-reactive, medium-sized saucepan. Place over low heat and stir to dissolve the sugar and honey. Add the ginger and slowly bring to simmering point. Turn off the heat and let the flavours infuse the vinegar.

When the jars are cool enough to handle, bring your brine back to simmering point. Using small clean tongs or clean hands, add some of the ginger from the brine to each jar, along with 2 orange peel strips, 4 allspice berries and 4 peppercorns. Carefully pack the rhubarb into the jars, then pour in the hot brine, making sure the rhubarb is completely submerged under the vinegar.

Remove any air bubbles by gently tapping each jar on the work surface and sliding a clean butterknife or chopstick around the inside to release any hidden air pockets. Wipe the rims of the jars with paper towel or a clean damp cloth and seal immediately.

For a firm texture, store in the fridge for up to 3 months. Or heat-process (see page 180) for 15 mins and store in the pantry for up to 6 months. The rhubarb will be ready to eat after 2 weeks, but will be better after 1 month. Once opened, refrigerate and use within 2 months.

6–8 rhubarb stalks

500 ml (17 fl oz/2 cups) red wine vinegar

330 g (11½ oz/1½ cups) raw sugar

250 ml (9 fl oz/1 cup) water

2 Tbsp honey

20 g (¾ oz) knob of fresh ginger, washed but not peeled, cut into slices about 1 cm (½ inch) thick

4–6 strips of orange peel

8–12 dried allspice berries

8–12 peppercorns

Winter

IN SEASON: Apple, beetroot, cabbage, carrot, cumquat, lemon, onion, pear, pumpkin

Preserved Lemons or Limes

PREPARATION TIME:
20 mins

STORAGE: **several years**

MAKES: **3–4 x 300 ml (10½ fl oz/1¼ cup) jars**

1 kg (2 lb 4 oz) lemons or limes – if using limes, you may need a few extra if they aren't particularly juicy

100–150 g (3½ –5½ oz) salt

FOR EACH JAR OF PRESERVED LEMONS, YOU WILL NEED:

1 bay leaf or 1 cinnamon stick and 2 cloves

1 dried allspice berry

5 black peppercorns

FOR EACH JAR OF PRESERVED LIMES, YOU WILL NEED:

1 red chilli

½ tsp coriander seeds

5 black peppercorns

Every home cook should know how to make preserved lemons or limes – they're the most straightforward and cheapest of all the preserves. All you need is lemons or limes and salt!

Once you have a jar of these on the go, you'll wonder how you lived without them: use to pep up a white bean mash or lamb tagine, stir through aïoli or smash into avocado and serve on toast.

Sterilise your jars and lids (see page 181), then leave to cool completely.

Cut the lemons or limes into quarters, or halves if very small. Put 1 tablespoon of salt into the bottom of each jar. Add a few layers of lemon or lime quarters into the jar, pressing down as you go to release the fruit's juices.

Slide your chosen spices down the side of each jar. Sprinkle with another layer of salt, then add another layer of lemon or lime quarters and repeat these layers until the jar is full. Remember to keep pushing down as you go. The fruit needs to be completely covered in salty juice – if your fruit hasn't released enough of its own juices, squeeze a few extra and pour in this juice to cover.

Leave 1 cm (½ inch) of space between the top of the fruit and the lid of the jar – you don't want the salty fruit touching the lid or it will corrode the metal. Seal the jars and let them sit in a cool, dark place for 6 weeks.

You know your lemons or limes are preserved when the salt has completely dissolved into a gel-like liquid. Preserved lemons and limes will keep for years, but opened jars are best stored in the fridge (if the top layer of fruit looks discoloured, just discard it and the rest should be fine to use).

Fermented Carrots

Follow these same steps to ferment any sturdy vegetables you have on hand: try beetroot (beets), radishes, kohlrabi, green beans, celery or cauliflower florets.

These are great tossed through a salad. They're also surprisingly sweet. If you're ever going to get a kid to eat fermented vegetables, this would be the place to start.

Make a brine by putting the water and salt into a non-reactive saucepan. Bring to the boil, then remove from the heat and leave to cool to room temperature.

Mix together your carrot, onion, turmeric and ginger.

Pack the carrot mixture into clean jars (see page 179 for more on packing techniques), then fill the jars with the brine until the vegetables are completely covered. Wipe the rims of the jars with paper towel or a clean damp cloth and seal.

Let the jars sit at room temperature, but out of direct sunlight, for 2–7 days. During this time, the lids will start to pop up, which is a sign of the fermenting process (see pages 184–185 for some fermenting tips). Open your jar every few days to 'burp' your ferment – this will release the built-up carbon dioxide, and prevent brine spilling out of the jar.

Transfer the jars to the fridge and leave for a week before using. Refrigerated, the fermented carrots will keep for up to 6 months.

PREPARATION TIME:
30 mins, plus 2–7 days fermenting

STORAGE: **up to 6 months in the fridge**

MAKES: **2 x 300 ml (10½ fl oz/1¼ cup) jars**

2 tsp salt

500 ml (17 fl oz/2 cups) water

500 g (1 lb 2 oz) carrots, thinly sliced

1 brown onion, thinly sliced

40 g (1½ oz) fresh turmeric, finely grated

40 g (1½ oz) grated fresh ginger

Choko Pickles

We've tried dozens of ways to use chokos (chayote), but we've decided that the best thing to do with them is to make pickles. Chokos don't have much flavour of their own, so they readily absorb whatever you put in with them. They maintain their shape and crunch in the jar, plus are still good after a year in the pantry. They're great with cheese and crackers, on a ham sandwich, or with oily fish.

PREPARATION TIME:
45 mins, plus at least
1–2 hours salting, plus
15 mins heat-processing

COOKING TIME: **10 mins**

STORAGE: **up to 1 year**

MAKES: **2 x 400 ml
(14 fl oz/1½ cup) jars**

**800 g (1 lb 12 oz) chokos
(chayote)**

1 Tbsp salt

**500 ml (17 fl oz/2 cups)
white wine vinegar**

**110 g (3¾ oz/½ cup) caster
(superfine) sugar**

¼ tsp ground turmeric

1 tsp salt

250 ml (9 fl oz/1 cup) water

2 lemon slices

2 garlic cloves

2 bay leaves

a few black peppercorns

If your chokos have been sitting on the vine for too long their skin gets tough, so it's better to peel the older ones. Cut the chokos into long thin strips, discarding the seeds and core, then put the strips into a bowl. Sprinkle with the salt, mix well with your hands and leave to sit for an hour or two (or overnight). This will draw out any excess moisture and help to keep the chokos crunchy. Transfer to a large colander and leave to drain thoroughly.

Meanwhile, sterilise your jars and lids (see page 181).

Make a brine by putting the vinegar, sugar, turmeric, salt and water into a non-reactive saucepan over low heat. Stir to dissolve the sugar, then increase the heat and bring to the boil.

When the jars are cool enough to handle, use small tongs or clean hands to carefully pack the drained chokos into the jars, adding a lemon slice, garlic clove, bay leaf and a couple of peppercorns to each jar. The jars should be full but not over-packed – the brine needs to cover every strip of choko, and if they are packed too tightly the brine won't be able to get into every nook and cranny (see page 179 for more on packing techniques).

Fill the jars with brine until the chokos are covered. Remove any air bubbles by gently tapping each jar on the work surface and sliding a butterknife or chopstick around the inside to release any hidden air pockets. You may need to add more brine or chokos after doing this (the liquid should reach about 1 cm/½ inch from the top of the jar). Wipe the rims of the jars with paper towel or a clean damp cloth and seal.

Heat-process (see page 180) for 15 mins, then store in a cool, dark place for up to 12 months. Once opened, refrigerate and use within a few months.

Pickled Cumquats

These were among the first pickles we ever made. Our neighbour had three huge cumquat trees in his yard, and when we asked what he did with them all, he gave us a list of the ways his family preserved them: as marmalade and syrup, and in salt, adding that the salted ones were very good for sore throats.

These cumquats were inspired by a Stephanie Alexander recipe, though we add cumin and peppercorns to ours. They're great in a stuffing for roast chicken and added to Moroccan-style stews. They're also amazing with stinky cheese.

Make a brine by putting the vinegar, sugar and water into a non-reactive saucepan over low heat. Stir to dissolve the sugar, then add the peppercorns and cumin seeds. Increase the heat and bring to the boil. Turn off the heat and let sit for about 15 mins.

Meanwhile, sterilise your jars and lids (see page 181).

Remove any stems from the cumquats. Bring the brine back to a simmer and, working in batches, slip the cumquats into the brine for a few mins to soften them slightly – when their skins turn glossy, they're ready. Use a slotted spoon to scoop them out, then set aside in a bowl.

When the jars are cool enough to handle, use small tongs or clean hands to carefully pack the cumquats into the jars, adding a cinnamon stick and a clove to each jar. You want to pack as many cumquats into each jar as possible without bursting the skins (see page 179 for more on packing techniques).

Fill the jars with brine until the cumquats are covered. Remove any air bubbles by gently tapping each jar on the work surface and sliding a butterknife or chopstick around the inside to release any hidden air pockets. You may need to add more brine or cumquats after doing this (the liquid should reach about 1 cm/½ inch from the top of the jar). Wipe the rims of the jars with paper towel or a clean damp cloth and seal.

Heat-process (see page 180) for 15 mins, then store in a cool, dark place. Let sit for at least a month before using. Once a jar is opened, store in the fridge and use within 6 months.

PREPARATION TIME:
20 mins, plus 20 mins sterilising, plus 15 mins heat-processing

STORAGE: up to 2 years

MAKES: 5 x 300 ml (10½ fl oz/1¼ cup) jars

1 litre (35 fl oz/4 cups) white wine vinegar

500 g (1 lb 2 oz) caster (superfine) sugar

500 ml (17 fl oz/2 cups) water

1 tsp black peppercorns

2 tsp cumin seeds

1.5 kg (3 lb 5 oz) cumquats

5 cinnamon sticks

5 cloves

Oven-Roasted Onion Relish

PREPARATION TIME:
10 mins

COOKING TIME: **1¼ hours**

STORAGE: **up to 2 weeks in the fridge**

MAKES: **200 g (7 oz/ 1½ cups)**

3 onions

60 ml (2 fl oz/¼ cup) apple cider vinegar

60 g (2¼ oz/¼ cup) brown sugar

1 Tbsp chopped herbs (such as rosemary or thyme)

½ tsp salt

½ tsp freshly ground black pepper

60 ml (2 fl oz/¼ cup) olive oil

This is for when you want onion relish at your barbecue but you don't want to stand around stirring a pot all afternoon. The onions are roasted in vinegar and sugar, and you can add spices and flavours to suit your meal. We've kept it simple with just herbs, salt and pepper here, but feel free to add ground cumin, cloves and cayenne pepper for more intensity.

Preheat the oven to 180°C (350°F). Slice the onions in half, then into 1 cm (½ inch) strips. Pop them in a casserole dish or other ovenproof dish and add the remaining ingredients. Mix well, cover with the lid or foil and cook in the oven for 60 mins. Remove the lid or foil and cook for another 15 mins, until the liquid has evaporated a little and the onion is browning at the edges.

Add a little more salt and pepper and serve either hot or at room temperature. Store in a clean jar or airtight container in the fridge for up to 2 weeks.

Beetskraut

Not really a sauerkraut as there's no cabbage here, but we are using the same method and making a fermented beetroot (beets) kraut that you can eat in the same way as a sauerkraut: on sandwiches, in salads and alongside grains, potatoes and roasted vegetables or meats. It's a great way to use the whole bunch of beetroot – roots, stems, leaves and all. This is not a beginner's ferment, not because it's difficult, but because the high sugar content of beetroot means they ferment quickly and can go slimy if you don't keep your eye on them. Make this in winter when beetroot is in season and fermentation takes a little longer. Allow for a maximum of 4 days to ferment before transferring to the fridge.

Cut the stems off the beetroot, then scrub the roots and wash the leaves and stems. Thinly slice the stems, shred the leaves (discarding any really big, gnarly ones) and put both in a bowl. Grate the roots into the bowl. Add the salt and your choice of flavourings. Mix well.

Using clean hands, massage all the ingredients until everything is quite wet and your hands are purple. Fill your clean jar, pressing down so the liquid rises above the beetroot and any air bubbles are released. Repeat this process until the jar is filled. The liquid must cover the beetroot by about 1 cm (½ inch). Wipe the rim of the jar with paper towel or a clean damp cloth and seal.

Now for fermentation: place your jar in a cool dry place for 2–4 days. In this time, your beetskraut will ferment and you'll notice it starting to bubble and perhaps some juice escaping. Simply wipe the jar down. If needed, open your jar to 'burp' the ferment – this will release the built-up carbon dioxide and prevent brine spilling out of the jar.

Store in the fridge for up to 3 months. The beetskraut may be eaten immediately but will improve with time (we suggest leaving it for at least 1 week).

PREPARATION TIME:
10 mins, plus 2–4 days fermenting

STORAGE: up to 3 months in the fridge

MAKES: 1 x 750 ml (26 fl oz/3 cup) jar (or a few smaller jars)

4 beetroot (beets)

3 tsp salt

2 Tbsp of any of the following: dill seeds, grated horseradish, finely chopped garlic, black peppercorns or mustard seeds

Piccalilli

PREPARATION TIME:
45 mins, plus 20 mins
sterilising, plus 10 mins
heat-processing

COOKING TIME: 10 mins

STORAGE: up to 1 year

MAKES: 4 x 300 ml
(10½ fl oz/1¼ cup) jars

350 g (12 oz) cauliflower
(about ¼ cauliflower), cut
into small florets

150 g (5½ oz) carrot (about
1 medium–large carrot),
thinly sliced

250 g (9 oz) fennel (about
¼ large or 1 small fennel
bulb), thinly sliced

250 g (9 oz) green beans,
cut into thirds

4 cloves

1 tsp fenugreek seeds

1 tsp black peppercorns

2 Tbsp brown mustard
seeds

250 ml (9 fl oz/1 cup) white
wine vinegar

250 ml (9 fl oz/1 cup) water

2 Tbsp cornflour
(cornstarch)

2 tsp salt

½ tsp ground turmeric

100 g (3½ oz/scant ½ cup)
caster (superfine) sugar

This English pickle is the perfect thing to take to a picnic.
We also add it to ham and cheese sandwiches and spoon some
onto our ploughman's plates.

You can use any vegetables you have on hand for this.
We make seasonal variations, depending on what's available.
Radish, zucchini (courgettes), choko (chayote), white cabbage,
daikon, thinly sliced Brussels sprouts, green chillies and
onion are all great to use – you need a kilogram (2 lb 4 oz) of
vegetables all up.

Bring a large saucepan of salted water to the boil. Add the
cauliflower florets and blanch for 1 minute, then drain and refresh
under cold running water. Mix the cauliflower and all the other
vegetables together.

Grind the cloves, fenugreek seeds, peppercorns and half of
the mustard seeds into a fine powder using a spice grinder.

Next, sterilise your jars and lids (see page 181).

Combine the vinegar with the water in a non-reactive saucepan.
In a large heatproof bowl, mix the cornflour, salt and turmeric with
the ground spices and the remaining mustard seeds, then stir in
60 ml (2 fl oz/¼ cup) of the vinegar mixture to make a smooth
paste. Add the sugar to the remaining vinegar mixture, then place
the pan over medium heat and stir until the sugar has dissolved.
Slowly pour the hot brine into the cornflour paste, whisking as you
go, to make a smooth, thick sauce. Add the vegetables and gently
stir through until they are evenly coated with the sauce.

Pack the hot piccalilli into the hot jars, seal and heat-process
(see page 180) for 10 mins. Store the jars in a cool, dark place
for at least a month before using. Unopened jars of piccalilli will
keep for up to 12 months. Once opened, refrigerate and use within
3 months.

Pickled Ginger Carrots

Gingery, tangy and spicy, these carrot pickles are delicious in noodle salads, tossed through stir-fries at the end or served on bibimbap. When pickling the carrots, you can also add thinly sliced daikon, radish or choko (chayote).

Make your brine by combining the vinegar, sugar, salt and water in a non-reactive, medium-sized saucepan. Place over low heat and stir to dissolve the sugar and salt. Add the chilli flakes and lemongrass, or lemon peel strips, and slowly bring to simmering point. Turn off the heat and let the brine sit so the flavours can develop.

Meanwhile, sterilise your jars and lids (see page 181).

Thinly slice the carrots, onion, spring onions and ginger, as well as any other vegetables you may be using, and tumble together in a bowl.

When the jars are cool enough to handle, carefully pack the carrot mixture into them, making sure you include a bit of lemongrass or lemon peel in each jar. Bring your brine back to the boil, then cover the vegetables with the hot brine.

Remove any air bubbles by gently tapping each jar on the work surface and sliding a clean butterknife or chopstick around the inside to release any hidden air pockets. Wipe the rims of the jars with paper towel or a clean damp cloth and seal immediately.

Leave to cool on the benchtop, then store in the fridge for up to 3 months. Leave to sit for at least 2 weeks before eating. Once opened, store in the fridge and consume within 6 months.

To extend the shelf life to up to 1 year, heat-process the jars (see page 180) for 15 mins, then store in a cool, dark place.

TIP: With preserving and pickling, it is important to use 100 per cent sea or river salt, without any additives. If your salt has added iodine, it can make the vinegar brine dark; if it contains an anticaking agent, it can make the brine cloudy.

PREPARATION TIME: 25 mins, plus 20 mins sterilising, plus 15 mins heat-processing (optional)

STORAGE: 3 months in the fridge, or up to 1 year if heat-processed

MAKES: 2–3 x 400 ml (14 fl oz/1½ cup) jars

500 ml (17 fl oz/2 cups) rice wine vinegar (with an acidity level of 5% or more)

55 g (2 oz/¼ cup) caster (superfine) sugar

2 tsp salt (see Tip)

250 ml (9 fl oz/1 cup) water

1 tsp chilli flakes

4 lemongrass stems, white part only, cut into 4 cm (1½ inch) lengths, or 4 strips of lemon peel

500 g (1 lb 2 oz) carrots, peeled

1 small brown onion

5 spring onions (scallions)

40 g (1½ oz) knob of fresh ginger, washed well

Pickled Beetroot

PREPARATION TIME:
**30 mins, plus 20 mins
sterilising, plus 15 mins
heat-processing**

STORAGE: **up to 2 years**

MAKES: **2–4 x 500 ml
(17 fl oz/2 cup) jars**

**1 kg (2 lb 4 oz) beetroot
(beet) bulbs (trimmed
weight: if your bunch has
stalks and leafy tops,
reserve these for pickling
– see Tip)**

**750 ml (26 fl oz/3 cups) red
wine vinegar**

**375 ml (13 fl oz/1½ cups)
water**

**110 g (3¾ oz/½ cup) white
sugar**

**50 g (1¾ oz/¼ cup) brown
sugar**

2 tsp salt

FOR EACH JAR,
YOU WILL NEED:

¼ tsp black peppercorns

1 tsp dill seeds or dried dill

You should definitely give this preserving recipe a go – you'll
never want to buy beetroot (beets) in a tin again. The pickled
beetroot is delicious thinly sliced in salads, on burgers or
with cheddar.

Sterilise your jars and lids (see page 181).

Meanwhile, wash and peel the beetroot, then slice them any way
you like – thin slices are great for burgers and sandwiches; wedges
work well for salads and cheese plates.

Make your brine by combining the vinegar, water, sugar and salt
in a non-reactive, medium-sized saucepan over low heat. Stir to
dissolve the sugar and salt. Bring to simmering point, then turn off
the heat.

When the jars are cool enough to handle, add the peppercorns
and dill. Using small tongs or clean hands, carefully but tightly
pack the beetroot pieces into the jars. Pour the hot brine over until
they are completely covered; any leftover brine can be stored in
the fridge for up to 1 month and used in salad dressings and other
pickles.

Remove any air bubbles by gently tapping each jar on the work
surface and sliding a clean butterknife or chopstick around the
inside to release any hidden air pockets. Wipe the rims of the jars
with paper towel or a clean damp cloth and seal immediately.

Heat-process the jars (see page 180) for 15 mins, then leave to
cool on the benchtop. Store in a cool, dark place for up to 2 years.

Leave to sit for at least 1 month before eating, although they will
be even better after 3 months; if you've pickled whole beets, or big
chunks, you'll need to let them sit longer. Once opened, store in the
fridge and use within 6 months.

TIP: Beetroot stems are excellent to add to any quick pickles.
If the leaves are in good condition, wash and dry them, then finely
slice and toss through a salad. At the Picklery, we even collect our
beetroot skins and give them to our friend Leah, who makes natural
dyes for fabrics!

Malt-Pickled Onions

These pickled onions are a good option in salads to add sweetness and bite. Unusually, there is no water in this pickling brine, as the onions have enough water in them already.

Plunge the whole onions in boiling water for 30 seconds, then run under cold water. Peel off the skins. Leave small onions whole and cut larger ones in half or quarters.

Put the onions in a large non-reactive bowl. Sprinkle with the salt and leave in the fridge overnight to draw out excess moisture.

The next day, make your brine by combining the vinegar, sugar, ginger and all the spices in a non-reactive, medium-sized saucepan over low heat. Stir to dissolve the sugar, bring to simmering point, then turn off the heat and let the flavours infuse the vinegar.

Meanwhile, sterilise your jars and lids (see page 181).

When the jars are cool enough to handle, rinse your onions under cold water to remove the salt, then drain well. Pack the onions firmly into the jars, leaving 1 cm (½ inch) space at the top.

Bring your brine back up to heat – it needs to be very hot before you pour it over the onions.

Pour the hot brine over the onions, evenly distributing the spices among the jars. Make sure the onions are completely submerged.

Remove any air bubbles by gently tapping each jar on the benchtop and sliding a clean butterknife or chopstick around the inside. Wipe the rims with paper towel or a clean damp cloth and seal immediately.

Leave to cool, then store in a cool, dark place for up to 1 year. The onions can be eaten after 4–6 weeks but will be better after 3 months. Once opened, store in the fridge for up to 6 months.

TIP: For lighter, tangier pickled onions, use apple cider vinegar instead of malt vinegar. Use 55 g (2 oz/¼ cup) white sugar and 50 g (1¾ oz/¼ cup) brown sugar. Leave out the star anise, cloves and cayenne pepper, and add 2 bay leaves to each jar with the ginger, allspice and mustard seeds.

PREPARATION TIME: 30 mins, plus overnight salting, plus 20 mins sterilising

STORAGE: **up to 1 year**

MAKES: **3–4 x 500 ml (17 fl oz/2 cup) jars**

1 kg (2 lb 4 oz) small brown onions

3 Tbsp salt

750 ml (26 fl oz/3 cups) malt vinegar

300 g (10½ oz/1½ cups) brown sugar

4 slices of well-washed fresh ginger

6 star anise

12 cloves

12 dried allspice berries

3 tsp yellow mustard seeds

¼ tsp cayenne pepper

Beet Relish

PREPARATION TIME:
15 mins

COOKING TIME: 30 mins

STORAGE: up to 2 months
in the fridge

MAKES: about 3 x 300 ml
(10½ fl oz/1¼ cup) jars

60 ml (2 fl oz/¼ cup)
sunflower or other
vegetable oil

1 onion, thinly sliced

a bunch of beetroot (beets)

1 apple, grated (leave it
out if you don't have it,
or replace it with 75 g/
2½ oz/1 cup shredded
cabbage)

1 tsp freshly ground black
pepper

2–3 Tbsp grated fresh
ginger or 1–2 tsp ground
cumin

500 ml (18 fl oz/2 cups) red
wine vinegar or apple cider
vinegar

110 g (3½ oz/½ cup) caster
(superfine) sugar

1–2 tsp salt

This is a good recipe for when you've bought a bunch of
beetroot (beets) and have no idea what to do with them. It's
simple to make, uses the whole bunch including stems, and
lasts for months in the fridge. Serve on sandwiches, burgers
and steaks, or with cheese or falafel.

In a medium saucepan, heat the oil over medium heat. Add the
onion and the thinly sliced beetroot stems and sauté until soft,
sweet and pink. Add 3–4 peeled and grated raw beetroot, the
grated apple, pepper and ginger or ground cumin. Add the vinegar,
sugar and salt.

Stir until the sugar dissolves, reduce the heat to low, then
simmer for 20 mins or until the relish has begun to thicken, adding
a little water if it starts to dry out.

Store in clean jars or an airtight container in the fridge for up to
2 months.

Carrot Kimchi

Kimchi is a living tradition, and kimchi recipes embrace produce that is both native to South Korea and introduced, resulting in a huge spectrum of this national condiment. This carrot kimchi is sweet and mild, so it might convert even those who are not fermenting enthusiasts.

Put the grated carrot in a non-reactive bowl and cover with water and the salt. Leave on the bench overnight. The next day, drain and rinse the carrot a few times in cold water. Transfer to a large bowl and add the leek, chilli flakes, sesame seeds, garlic and ginger.

Pack the mixture into a clean jar, pressing down as you go and making sure the water that's released is 1 cm (½ inch) above the carrot at the top of the jar. Seal and leave to ferment at room temperature (out of direct sunlight) for 2–4 days, then transfer to the fridge for another 4 days. After this time, your carrot kimchi will be ready to eat. Store in the fridge for up to 6 months. (See pages 184–185 for more fermenting tips.)

PREPARATION TIME:
15 mins, plus overnight salting, plus 2–4 days fermenting

STORAGE: up to 6 months in the fridge

MAKES: 1 x 500 ml (17 fl oz/2 cup) jar

500 g (1 lb 2 oz) carrot, grated

2 tsp salt

1 small leek, thinly sliced

1 tsp chilli flakes

1 Tbsp sesame seeds

1 Tbsp minced garlic

1 Tbsp minced fresh ginger

Sticky Onion Worcestershire Relish

PREPARATION TIME:
40 mins, plus 20 mins sterilising, plus 10 mins heat-processing

COOKING TIME: **about 2¼ hours**

STORAGE: **up to 2 years if heat-processed**

MAKES: **3–4 x 300 ml (10½ fl oz/1¼ cup) jars**

80 ml (2½ fl oz/⅓ cup) olive or vegetable oil

1.5 kg (3 lb 5 oz) onion, thinly sliced

1 Tbsp salt

½ tsp ground cloves

½ tsp ground allspice

½ tsp ground star anise

½ tsp freshly ground black pepper

½ tsp ground cinnamon

½ tsp freshly grated nutmeg

¼ tsp cayenne pepper

40 g (1½ oz) grated fresh ginger

500 ml (17 fl oz/2 cups) malt vinegar

250 ml (9 fl oz/1 cup) water

115 g (4 oz/⅓ cup) molasses

250 g (9 oz/1¼ cups) brown sugar

zest and juice of 1 lemon

Sticky and very rich in flavour, this relish needs to be cooked for a long time to get the right consistency and colour, but it's well worth it. Make sure you sauté the onion down in batches, or you'll end up with a soupy pot of oniony liquid.

Serve this relish on a ploughman's plate or a toasted sandwich, or use a few tablespoons in a marinade for meats.

Find a large, non-reactive saucepan – for even evaporation, it's better to use a wider and shallower pan than a stockpot.

Heat the oil in the saucepan over medium heat. Add half the onion and half the salt. Slowly soften for about 15 mins, stirring often, until the onion is starting to collapse. Now stir in the remaining onion and cook, stirring often, for about 20 mins, until all the onion is evenly cooked, and the liquid has evaporated – you don't want the onions stewing in their own juices.

Stir in all the spices and ginger and gently cook for about 5 mins, until fragrant, stirring constantly. Add all the remaining ingredients, including the remaining salt, stirring to dissolve the sugar.

Gently cook over low heat for up to 1½ hours, stirring often to prevent sticking, until the relish is glossy and sticky. When your onion relish is ready there will be no vinegar pooling on the surface, and you should be able to run your spoon through the centre and see the bottom of the pan.

Meanwhile, sterilise your jars and lids (see page 181).

Carefully fill the hot jars with the hot relish. Remove any air bubbles by gently tapping each jar on the work surface and sliding a clean butterknife or chopstick around the inside to release any hidden air pockets. Wipe the rims of the jars with paper towel or a clean damp cloth and seal immediately.

Heat-process the jars (see page 180) for 10 mins, then store in a cool, dark place for up to 2 years. Once opened, store in the fridge and use within 6 months.

PRESERVING AND PICKLING IS THE PERFECT WAY TO
EXTRACT MAXIMUM FLAVOUR FROM THE PARTS OF THE
INGREDIENT THAT WOULD GENERALLY END UP IN THE BIN.

Kitchen Scrap Sauerkraut

PREPARATION TIME:
**40 mins, plus 2 days–
2 weeks fermenting time**

STORAGE: **up to 6 months
in the fridge**

MAKES: **3–4 x 500 ml
(17 fl oz/2 cup) jars**

**1.5 kg (3 lb 5 oz) white
cabbage**

**500 g (1 lb 2 oz) assorted
leftover fruit and vegetable
bits, such as onions,
apples, pears, chokos
(chayotes), kohlrabi,
chopped parsley, dill,
beetroot (beet), fennel,
kale and celery**

1½ Tbsp salt

**1 Tbsp whole spices
of your choice, such
as juniper berries,
caraway seeds, bay
leaves and black or white
peppercorns**

This sauerkraut recipe (pictured on the following pages) comes from Cornersmith's head fermenter and teacher, Jaimee Edwards. It's a very flexible one in which you can use up vegetable stems and leaves, or those bits lurking in the back of the fridge. All together you'll need 2 kg (4 lb 8 oz) of produce, including 500 g (1 lb 2 oz) fruit and veggie 'scraps'.

Flavour the sauerkraut with whole spices or herbs to match your vegetable combinations. Caraway seeds are a classic with cabbage, apple and onion; black peppercorns go well with fennel and beetroot; and kale and dill are really delicious together.

You can quarter or halve the recipe if you only want to make 1 or 2 jars.

Cut the cabbage into manageable pieces and shred any smaller portions of cabbage into thin strips. Put it in a non-reactive bowl large enough to hold all your produce.

If you are using apples or pears, cut them into thin strips and set aside. Cut your other vegetables and greens to about the same size as your cabbage, then add them to the bowl.

Sprinkle the salt on the cabbage mixture and mix thoroughly with your hands. Using a pestle, or a rolling pin without a handle – or even the top side of a meat mallet – pound your produce until a lot of the water is released. You should be able to grab a fist full of the mixture, give it a squeeze, and see brine running freely. At this stage your sauerkraut is ready to put into jars. If you are using apples or pears, mix them through now. Taste the cabbage, adding salt if needed.

Put the sauerkraut into clean jars and pack down very tightly, to about 2 cm (¾ inch) from the rim of the jars, allowing about 1 cm (½ inch) of the brine from your produce to cover the top of the mixture. This is very important to prevent spoilage.

Seal your jars and place them out of direct sunlight. In temperate weather, leave to ferment for at least 4 days; in summer, it is advisable to check on your sauerkraut after 2 days, as fermentation will happen much more quickly.

Open your jar every few days to 'burp' your ferment – this will release the built-up carbon dioxide and prevent brine spilling out of the jar. Just be sure to press down your sauerkraut afterwards, so that the brine is covering the top by at least 1 cm (½ inch).

You may leave your sauerkraut to ferment for 2 weeks, checking every few days to see and taste how it is developing. Once you are happy with your sauerkraut, refrigerate for up to 6 months.

Pear, Lemon & Rosemary Chutney

A versatile chutney that is as equally at home with meats or in a sandwich as it is on a ploughman's plate. You need pears that are full of flavour and on the riper side for this. We don't usually peel the fruit for this country-style chutney as we like it to retain some texture, but if you want a smoother consistency, peel the pears and cut them into smaller chunks.

We've suggested red wine vinegar here for a richer, more wintry feel, but apple cider vinegar also works, as does a mix of pears and apples.

Heat the vegetable oil in a large heavy-based saucepan over low to medium heat. Sauté the onion until soft but not browned. Stir in the pear, salt, pepper and cloves, along with half of the lemon zest and half of the rosemary, and cook until the pears soften slightly.

Add the vinegar and sugar. Stir until the sugar has dissolved, then increase the heat to medium. Cook the chutney, stirring regularly to stop it sticking, for a good hour or so, until the desired consistency is reached: the chutney should be glossy and thick, with no puddles of liquid on the surface. Stir through the rest of the rosemary and cook for another 5 mins. Taste and add more lemon zest or salt, if needed, then set aside to cool for 10 mins.

Meanwhile, sterilise your jars and lids (see page 181).

Carefully ladle the hot chutney into the hot jars. Wipe the rims of the jars with paper towel or a clean damp cloth and seal immediately.

Heat-process the jars (see page 180) for 10 mins, then store in cool, dark place for up to 12 months, leaving the chutney to sit for at least 6 weeks before using. Once opened, store in the fridge and use within 3 months.

PREPARATION TIME:
45 mins, plus 10 mins heat-processing

COOKING TIME: **2 hours**

STORAGE: **up to 1 year**

MAKES: **5 x 300 ml (10½ fl oz/1¼ cup) jars**

80 ml (2½ fl oz/⅓ cup) vegetable oil

500 g (1 lb 2 oz) onion, thinly sliced

2 kg (4 lb 8 oz) ripe pears, cut into 2 cm (¾ inch) cubes

2 tsp salt

1 tsp freshly ground black pepper

4 cloves

finely grated zest of 1 lemon

1 rosemary sprig, leaves picked and finely chopped

600 ml (21 fl oz/2½ cups) red wine vinegar

250 g (9 oz/generous 1 cup) caster (superfine) sugar

Sweet Pickled Pears

PREPARATION TIME:
**30 mins, plus 20 mins
sterilising, plus 15 mins
heat-processing**

STORAGE: **up to 2 years**

MAKES: **3–4 x 500 ml
(17 fl oz/2 cup) jars**

**500 ml (17 fl oz/2 cups)
apple cider vinegar**

250 ml (9 fl oz/1 cup) water

**300 g (10½ oz/1½ cups)
brown sugar**

8 cloves

16 black peppercorns

12 dried allspice berries

4 bay leaves

**1 kg (2 lb 4 oz) firm pears,
washed**

Rich and sweet, these pickled pears are amazing with cheeses, or tossed through salads. We like to use firm green-skinned pears, but any pears are okay as long as they are very firm. Leaving the skin on helps the pickles hold their shape. They make a great addition to the Christmas table, especially with ham (and they make great gifts).

These pickles are lovely after a month. Once you've had a chance to enjoy them, don't throw the syrupy brine away – it's amazing in a cocktail or as the base in a salad dressing.

Sterilise your jars and lids (see page 181).

Meanwhile, make your pickling brine by combining the vinegar, water, sugar and spices in a non-reactive, medium-sized saucepan over low heat. Stir to dissolve the sugar, then bring to simmering point.

Cut the pears into halves or quarters and pack firmly into the jars, leaving 1 cm (½ inch) space at the top.

Bring your brine to the boil. Pour the hot brine over the pears, evenly distributing the spices among the jars, and ensuring the pears are completely submerged.

Remove any air bubbles by gently tapping each jar on the work surface and sliding a clean butterknife or chopstick around the inside to release any hidden air pockets. Wipe the rims of the jars with paper towel or a clean damp cloth and seal immediately.

Heat-process the jars (see page 180) for 15 mins, then store in a cool, dark place for up to 2 years. Once opened, store in the fridge and use within 6 months.

TIP: If your pears are really hard, you can soften them in the simmering vinegar brine for 10 mins. You can also make this recipe with peeled and quartered quinces – simmer them until lightly pink and starting to soften, then pickle as above.

Pumpkin &
Sesame Chutney

This chutney is very versatile – serve it with eggs and on wraps, and it's great as a table condiment.

Preheat the oven to 180°C (350°F).

Prepare the pumpkin by removing the skin, core and seeds. Cut the flesh into 5 cm (2 inch) chunks, place on a baking tray with 60 ml (2 fl oz/¼ cup) of the oil and ½ teaspoon of the salt. Bake for 40 mins, or until soft and caramelised.

Warm the remaining oil in a large, shallow and wide non-reactive saucepan over medium heat and sauté the onion, stirring often, for about 8 mins, or until soft and translucent. Add the garlic and ginger. Stir in the mustard seeds, cumin, cayenne pepper and sesame seeds and cook for a few mins.

Mix the roasted pumpkin through; it will fall apart as you do this. Add all the sugar, the vinegar and remaining salt. Stir to combine, then reduce the heat and cook for 15–20 mins, stirring often. Because the pumpkin is already cooked, this chutney won't take long to reach the right consistency. It should be thick, with no puddles of vinegar on the surface – you'll be able to run your spoon through and see the bottom of the pan for a few seconds. If it's too dry, you can loosen it up by stirring in a little more vinegar or water.

Meanwhile, sterilise your jars and lids (see page 181).

Carefully fill the hot jars with the hot relish. Remove any air bubbles by gently tapping each jar on the work surface and sliding a clean butterknife or chopstick around the inside to release any hidden air pockets. Wipe the rims of the jars with paper towel or a clean damp cloth and seal immediately.

Heat-process the jars (see page 180) for 10 mins. Leave to cool on the benchtop, then store in a cool, dark place for up to 2 years. Try to let the chutney sit for 1 month before eating. Once opened, store in the fridge and use within 6 months.

PREPARATION TIME:
30 mins, plus 20 mins sterilising, plus 10 mins heat-processing

COOKING TIME: 1 hour

STORAGE: up to 2 years

MAKES: 4–5 x 300 ml (10½ fl oz/1¼ cup) jars

2 kg (4 lb 8 oz) sweet pumpkin (winter squash), such as Jap or Kent; all up you'll need 1.5 kg (3 lb 5 oz) pumpkin flesh

125 ml (4 fl oz/½ cup) vegetable oil

2 tsp salt

500 g (1 lb 2 oz) onion, thinly sliced

2 garlic cloves, crushed

40 g (1½ oz) grated fresh ginger

2 tsp black mustard seeds

1 tsp ground cumin

¼ tsp cayenne pepper

1 Tbsp sesame seeds, toasted

110 g (3¾ oz/½ cup) white sugar

50 g (1¾ oz/¼ cup) brown sugar

500 ml (17 fl oz/2 cups) apple cider vinegar

Quick Banana & Coconut Chutney

PREPARATION TIME:
15 mins

COOKING TIME: **20 mins**

STORAGE: **up to 1 month in the fridge**

MAKES: **2 x 250 ml (9 fl oz/ 1 cup) jars**

3 Tbsp vegetable oil

1 onion, finely chopped

1 tsp salt, plus extra to taste

1 Tbsp grated fresh ginger

½ tsp ground turmeric

1 tsp mustard seeds

1 tsp cumin seeds

1 tsp chilli flakes

a pinch of cayenne pepper

400–500 g (14 oz– 1 lb 2 oz/2 cups) roughly chopped overripe banana

100 ml (3½ fl oz/scant ½ cup) apple cider vinegar or white wine vinegar

2 Tbsp caster (superfine) sugar

45 g (1½ oz/½ cup) desiccated coconut

This fast-cooking chutney is a great condiment to serve with curries, grilled fish, rice and lentils, and tastes wonderful with a bitey cheddar on rye.

Heat the vegetable oil in a saucepan over medium heat. Add the onion and salt and sauté for 4–5 mins, until the onion is soft and sweet. Add the grated ginger, turmeric, mustard seeds, cumin seeds, chilli flakes and cayenne pepper.

Sauté until fragrant, then add the banana, vinegar and sugar. Simmer over medium heat for 5–8 mins, stirring often, until the chutney starts to thicken. Add the desiccated coconut and mix well. Taste and add more salt or chilli if needed. Simmer for another minute or two until the chutney is thick and glossy, then allow to cool and store in a jar or airtight container in the fridge for up to 1 month. It tastes even better after a few days!

Banana Ketchup

PREPARATION TIME:
20 mins, plus 20 mins
sterilising, plus 15 mins
heat-processing (optional)

COOKING TIME: 30 mins

STORAGE: up to 2 months
in the fridge, or up to 2
years if heat-processed

MAKES: 2–3 250 ml
(9 fl oz/1 cup) bottles

3–4 ripe bananas, sliced
(about 350 g/12 oz)

1 onion, roughly chopped

3 garlic cloves

3 cm (1¼ inch) knob of
fresh ginger (optional)

1–2 chillies, chopped
or 1 tsp chilli flakes

330 ml (11¼ fl oz/1⅓ cups)
apple cider vinegar or
white wine vinegar

½ tsp salt

2–3 Tbsp vegetable oil

250 ml (9 fl oz/1 cup) apple
cider vinegar

1 Tbsp soy sauce

75 g (2½ oz/⅓ cup)
brown sugar

1 Tbsp mixed ground
spices (whatever you have
in the pantry – cinnamon,
allspice, ginger, cloves,
nutmeg, pepper)

Don't knock it till you've tried it. This condiment is huge in the
Philippines, where it's served with fried rice, chicken dishes and
grilled eggplant (broiled aubergine). You can use it as you would
other ketchups and sauces – on sausages, fries, meatloaf and
fish fingers – and it's perfect for using up overripe bananas.

Put the bananas, onion, garlic cloves, ginger (if using) chilli, 80 ml
(2½ fl oz/⅓ cup) of the vinegar and the salt into a food processor
or blender and blitz until smooth.

Heat the vegetable oil in a saucepan and add the banana
mixture, another 1 cup (250 ml) of vinegar, soy sauce, brown sugar
and mixed ground spices. Simmer for 20–30 mins over low heat,
adding 2–3 tablespoons of water if the ketchup gets too thick
or starts to stick to the pan. Once it's thick and glossy, pour into
bottles, seal well and store in the fridge for up to 2 months.

If you want to store this in the pantry for up to 2 years, pour the
hot ketchup into hot sterilised jars or bottles (see page 181), seal
and heat-process (see page 180) for 15 mins.

Sweet & Sour Quick Mandarin Relish

This one is good for those mandarins that tricked you – looking delicious on the outside but tasting like mattress foam on the inside. Serve with chicken, pork sausages and cheese plates, or stir a few tablespoons through couscous, a grain salad or slow-cooked dishes.

In a small saucepan, combine the sugar, water and apple cider vinegar. Warm gently over low heat to dissolve the sugar, then add the salt and pepper, spice of your choice and cayenne or chilli flakes. Turn up the heat and let the syrup simmer for 5 mins, until a little sticky. Add the mandarins, then cook, stirring well and often, until glossy and caramelised.

Store in a clean jar or airtight container in the fridge for up to 3 weeks.

PREPARATION TIME: **10 mins**

COOKING TIME: **15 mins**

STORAGE: **up to 3 weeks in the fridge**

MAKES: **1 x 250 ml (9 fl oz/ 1 cup) jar**

55 g (2 oz/¼ cup) caster (superfine) sugar

60 ml (2 fl oz/¼ cup) water

60 ml (2 fl oz/¼ cup) apple cider vinegar

½ tsp salt

½ tsp black pepper

1 tsp of a spice you like (fennel seeds, grated fresh ginger, ground cumin)

a pinch of cayenne pepper or chilli flakes

3 mandarins, peeled and roughly chopped (any seeds removed)

Rescued
Apple Chutney

We used to make this chutney a lot when the kids were little, using up all the apples from the fruit bowl with only one little bite taken out. This recipe is a good way to rescue fruit that is floury, bruised or wrinkled. Try it with pears, plums or even pumpkin (squash). Change the spices to whatever you have in the pantry.

Heat the oil in a saucepan over medium heat and sauté the onion (or that half onion leftover in the fridge) with the salt until soft and sweet. Add the mustard seeds, cinnamon, cloves, cayenne and ginger. Mix well, then throw in the apples, vinegar and sugar.

Reduce the heat and gently simmer until you have a thick and glossy chutney (add a little water if the chutney starts to look dry). Taste and add extra spices or sugar if needed. Allow to cool a little, then spoon into an airtight container or clean jar and store in the fridge for up to 1 month.

PREPARATION TIME: 15 mins

COOKING TIME: 20 mins

STORAGE: up to 1 month in the fridge

MAKES: 1 x 500 ml (17 fl oz/2 cup) jar

3 Tbsp olive, sunflower or vegetable oil

1 small onion, thinly sliced

1 tsp salt

1 tsp brown or yellow mustard seeds

½ tsp ground cinnamon

a pinch of ground cloves (or use 2 whole cloves)

a pinch of cayenne pepper

1–2 Tbsp grated fresh ginger

3 apples, roughly chopped with the skin on

125 ml (4 fl oz/½ cup) red wine vinegar, white wine vinegar or apple cider vinegar

55g (2 oz/¼ cup) sugar of your choice

Vietnamese-Style Pickles Using One Carrot

PREPARATION TIME:
10 mins

STORAGE: **up to 3 weeks in the fridge**

MAKES: **1 x 300 ml (10½ fl oz/1¼ cup) jar**

1 carrot

a radish, bit of cabbage or the end of a knob of ginger

1 tsp salt

1 Tbsp caster (superfine) sugar

125 ml (4 fl oz/½ cup) boiling water

125 ml (4 fl oz/½ cup) white wine vinegar or rice wine vinegar

If you've got one tired carrot left in the fridge, make a batch of these fridge pickles, which are based on the Vietnamese pickles used in banh mi. They can be ready in 10 mins and are perfect in salad rolls, fried rice, noodles and rice paper rolls.

Cut the carrot into matchsticks and pop it into a bowl. If you have a lonely radish, a bit of cabbage or the end of a knob of ginger, thinly slice them and add to the bowl. Sprinkle with the salt and sugar and mix with your hands.

Let the mixture sit for 5 mins, then cover with the boiling water and vinegar. Leave for 20 mins and then enjoy as soon as you like. These pickles will be fine for a few weeks in the fridge, if they last that long.

Pickling Guide

A love for pickling started the Cornersmith adventure, and it became our signature. You'll never get sick of having a pantry full of home-made pickled vegetables for salads, burgers, sandwiches, cheese plates or just to eat straight from the jar.

Once you understand the craft of pickling, it's really easy and fun. You don't need to make huge batches of pickles to last the whole winter; just start off making a few jars at a time and get your head around the process. Once you get the pickling bug, you can conquer the school fete and all your Christmas gifts.

The formula for making pickles is basically always the same. You just have to decide what you're going to pickle; how you're going to prepare the vegetable or fruit; and then which vinegar, sugar and spices you want to use.

WHAT TO PICKLE

Really you can pickle anything. There are a few things I wouldn't recommend – starchy foods such as bananas and potatoes are a bit gross. But as you can see throughout this book, most other vegetables and fruits are delicious pickled.

Our one rule is NEVER pickle anything that is out of season. Vegetables and fruits that are at the height of their season are the most delicious, the freshest and the cheapest. Never buy something imported or frozen to preserve with. It defeats the whole purpose!

For crunchy, tart pickles you need to choose small, freshly picked, firm vegetables that will maintain their texture. This is especially important when pickling fruits. You'll get the best results with very firm unripe fruits – green plums and mangoes, hard pears, etc.

As we're big believers in preserving what is left in the fridge at the end of the week, you can use produce that is starting to deteriorate or soften to make chutneys or relishes, or if you have a couple of wrinkly eggplants (aubergines) or an ageing cauliflower you didn't get to, you can roast them first and then pickle them. Check out the recipe for pickling roasted eggplant on page 77.

PREPARING YOUR VEGETABLES

Once you've decided what you're going to pickle, there are a few ways to prepare your vegetables to get them ready.

Produce with a high water content, such as cucumbers, zucchini (courgettes), green tomatoes and chokos (chayote), needs to be salted before you start pickling. The salt draws out excess moisture and helps keep your pickles crunchy. It's important to use granulated salt, with no iodine or anticaking agents that can make your brine dark and cloudy.

Sliced pickles, also known as 'bread and butter' pickles, should be salted for a few hours, while whole vegetables such as gherkins or baby zucchini need to be salted overnight. After salting, discard the liquid that has been drawn out of the vegetables. You shouldn't need to rinse the vegetables, but if you've been heavy-handed with the salting, by all means give them a quick rinse and then drain well.

Denser vegetables such as green beans, chillies, celery, beetroot (beets) and carrots can be sliced and put raw straight into the jar. This is the same for most fruits – except quinces, which need to be poached or roasted before they are pickled.

You can also char, smoke or roast vegetables to intensify the flavour. See page 25 for charred jalapeños and page 48 for pickled roasted fennel. This style of pickling is more like classic antipasto, great for picnics and shared plates.

Some vegetables and fruits might need a quick blanch before you pickle them. Cumquats should be slightly softened in their brine before they go into the jar. Whole beetroots will need a couple of mins in boiling water to soften them slightly before pickling. Garlic needs 10 seconds in boiling water to stop it turning blue as it sits in the vinegar brine.

MAKING A BRINE

Your brine is very important. It not only stops bacteria from growing but is also the difference between an average and a delicious pickle. When you're starting out, here's a basic ratio that really works for everything: 4 parts vinegar and 2 parts water to 1 part sugar (4:2:1), plus salt to taste. Once you get a bit more confident with pickling, you'll want to make

different brines to match different vegetables and fruits. In this book, I've given you lots of different brine ideas. Start experimenting and find the one you like the most.

It's important you match the vinegar to the produce – so, fruits are great in an apple cider vinegar; white wine vinegar is great for green vegetables and anything you want to maintain the colour and flavour of; red wine vinegar is delicious with beetroot, cherries and red grapes; rice wine vinegar is a good choice for ginger, radish or any Asian style of pickle; and malt vinegar is lovely with onions.

The better quality your vinegar, the better your pickles will be. But you don't need to buy the most expensive vinegar. Instead, try to find mid-range white and red wine vinegars you can buy in larger quantities. Note that vinegar for pickling needs to have an acidity of 5 per cent or higher – this should be indicated on the label. Please avoid straight-up white vinegar. It's so astringent and is really best for cleaning your bathroom!

The sugar you use in your pickles also is important. White or caster (superfine) sugar has no colour or flavour and really is best for pickling vegetables. You want the sugar to soften the acidity of the vinegar, not taste sweet. Don't get stressed about using sugar in pickles. The sugar levels might seem high in a whole recipe, but remember these are condiments, and generally you consume only a tablespoon or two at a sitting, not four jars! Raw sugar is lovely with fruit pickles, and we use brown sugar in our pickled pears and pickled onions. Most other sugars, such as rapadura or coconut sugar, are too strong in flavour and will overpower the pickle.

Remember that sugar alternatives such as honey, stevia and agave can be used as sweeteners, but they're not preserving agents and do not keep bacteria at bay.

To make your brine, put the vinegar, water, sugar and salt (or if you are pickling fruits, you can leave the salt out) in a non-reactive saucepan, stirring over low heat to dissolve the sugar. Bring to the boil and let the brine simmer for a few mins, then turn off the heat.

The flavouring that you add to your pickles is entirely up to you. Remember, it has nothing to do with the preserving process, so feel free to get creative. Whole dried spices such as mustard seeds, fennel seeds, dill seeds and peppercorns are the classic pickle spices, but try different combinations too. You can add a stick of cinnamon and strip of lemon peel, or a garlic clove and a sprig of rosemary and thyme from the garden. We always recommend a few teaspoons of a few different spices in each jar. Be mindful that the flavours you put in will develop over time; two cloves, a cinnamon stick and a few peppercorns will be delicious, whereas 12 cloves and a tablespoon of peppercorns will be pretty overpowering after a few weeks! Also try to avoid using ground spices, as they make the brine cloudy.

If you have any pickling brine left over, you can store it in a jar in the fridge for up to a month, and use it as a base in salad dressings and for quick pickling.

PACKING PICKLES INTO JARS

Packing fruit or vegetables perfectly into jars takes practice. You want to get in as much as possible, but without squashing or bruising, or bursting their skins, so you need a firm hand but a gentle touch. Aim to fill the jars to just below the rim, leaving enough room for the vegetables to be completely covered in brine without touching the lid.

Slowly pour the hot brine over the vegetables, making sure they're completely submerged (anything left uncovered will discolour and deteriorate, and could potentially go mouldy). It's important to get rid of any air bubbles from the jars before sealing them, or the pickles may spoil, because the oxygen in the bubbles enables microorganisms to thrive. To do this, gently tap each jar on the work surface and slide a clean butterknife or chopstick around the inside of the jar to release any hidden air pockets – you will see bubbles being released from in between the pickles. You may need to add more vegetables or brine afterwards. There needs to be a gap of 5 mm–1.5 cm (¼–⅝ inch) between the brine and the lid – this is called 'headspace', and it allows the vegetables to expand as they absorb the brine. Keep in mind that smaller and sliced vegetables will absorb less brine than larger ones, so adjust the headspace accordingly.

STORAGE

Wipe the rims of the jars with paper towel or a clean damp cloth, then put the lids on. If you plan to store your pickles for an extended period, I suggest you heat-process them. Pickles that have been heat-processed and stored correctly – in a cool, dark place – will last for up to 2 years unopened. Make sure you stick to any recommended storage times given in specific recipes. If you don't want to heat-process your pickles, you'll need to store them in the fridge and use them up within a month.

The advantage of heat-processing is that pickles get better over time. Whole pickles need to sit in their jars for at least 6 weeks before use but will taste even better after 6 months. Sliced pickles are ready after 2 weeks and are best eaten within 6 months, before their texture starts to deteriorate. Once opened, all pickles should be refrigerated, but will still last for many months in your fridge.

HEAT-PROCESSING
Also called 'water bathing' or 'canning', this process uses heat to stop the growth of bacteria. It generates pressure inside the preserving jar or bottle, which forces out any oxygen, creating an uninhabitable environment for microorganisms.

Treating your preserves in this way has two benefits: it lengthens their shelf life, and it ensures the jars or bottles are sealed correctly. Opinions differ on when heat-processing is necessary, but at Cornersmith we encourage our students to heat-process any cold-packed preserves, pickles and bottled fruit – as well as large batches of chutneys and jams that will be stored for some time.

Get the biggest pan you have, such as a stockpot – the taller, the better – and put it on the stovetop. Lay a folded tea towel (dish towel) in the bottom of the pan, then sit your jars on the tea towel, taking care not to cram them in, and keeping them clear of the sides

of the pan. (All these measures are to stop the jars from wobbling around and cracking as the water boils.) Roughly match the water temperature to the temperature of the jars (to help prevent breakages from thermal shock), then pour in enough water to cover the jars, either completely or at least until three-quarters submerged. Bring to the boil over medium heat. The heat-processing times given in the recipes start from boiling point, and will generally be 10–15 mins for jars or bottles up to 500 ml (17 fl oz/2 cup) capacity, or 20 mins for larger capacities.

You might have one or two breakages when you're starting out – the worst that can happen is that the remaining jars will swim in pickles for the rest of the processing time. Just keep going, then take the surviving jars out at the end and give them a wipe down. If they all break, you have our permission to have a gin and a lie down!

Once the heat-processing time is up, the lids should be puffed up and convex. Carefully remove the hot jars from the water. If you've bought some clamps, now is the time to use them, or you can use oven mitts and a thick cloth to protect your hands.

Line your jars up on the benchtop and let them sit overnight. As they cool, a vacuum will form inside each jar and suck down the lid, sealing them securely. In the morning, the lids should be concave: either get down to eye level with the top of the jar to check for the telltale dip in the lid, or lay a pencil across each lid to show the cavity below it.

If you have concerns about the seal of any of your jars (sometimes a couple of jars fail to seal correctly), store them in the fridge and use their contents within a few weeks.

WHICH JARS TO USE

When you're starting out, just use what you've got in the kitchen cupboard. Second-hand jars are fine, as long as there are no cracks or chips in the glass that could harbour micro-organisms or cause the jar to break when heated. Second-hand metal (but not plastic) lids are okay too, if they are in good condition. Make sure there is no rust, and that the white acid-proof coating inside the lids is intact. Also check that the lids aren't misshapen or dented, as both of these can interfere with the seal.

Jars with shoulders or a neck are best for pickling because these help to keep the contents submerged under the brine – you want to avoid vegetables floating to the top and not preserving properly. Also, make sure your jars are tightly packed to keep your pickles under the brine.

If you decide to buy new jars, get good-quality ones made of thick glass – we'd recommend going to a kitchen-supply shop and buying 20 jars and 40 lids. Cheap jars from discount stores often have thin glass, which tends to become brittle and break at high temperatures.

STERILISING JARS AND BOTTLES

To sterilise jars or bottles, give them a wash in hot soapy water and a good rinse, then place them upright in a baking dish in a cold oven. Heat the oven to 110°C (225°F) and, once it has reached temperature, leave the jars in the oven for about 10–15 mins, or until completely dry, then remove them carefully.

For hot packing, pour the hot chutney straight into the hot jars; for cold packing, let the jars cool before adding your pickles or preserves.

To sterilise the lids, place them in a large saucepan of boiling water for 5 mins, then drain and dry with clean paper towels, or leave them on a wire rack to air dry. Make sure they are completely dry before using.

IF YOU REGULARLY MAKE SMALL BATCHES OF CHUTNEY, PICKLES
AND SAUCES WITH LEFTOVER FRUIT AND VEGETABLES, YOU'LL
NOT ONLY HAVE A PANTRY FULL OF DELICIOUS CONDIMENTS,
YOU'LL ALSO REDUCE WHAT GOES INTO YOUR BIN EACH WEEK
AND CUT BACK YOUR OVERALL HOUSEHOLD FOOD BUDGET.

Fermenting Guide

Our resident fermenter, Jaimee Edwards, is passionate about the benefits of fermented foods, and here she generously shares her guide to the process, so you can try your hand at fermenting at home.

Fermented foods offer a rich variety of flavours and are beneficial to the health of your gut. They are also very simple to make at home; all you need is seasonal produce, salt and time.

Lacto-fermentation is a very safe method of food preservation. During lacto-fermentation, the lactic acid–producing bacteria (lactobacilli) present on the surface of all vegetables and fruit are encouraged to proliferate in an anaerobic (oxygen-free) environment. Salt is used to inhibit the growth of any harmful bacteria for a few days while the 'good' lactobacilli generate enough lactic acid to preserve the fruit and vegetables. Salt should always be used, at a ratio of about 30 g (1 oz) fine salt to 2 kg (4 lb 8 oz) produce.

Preparing fermented vegetables and fruit is very easy, but once they are packed into their jars you will need to keep an eye on them. Carbon dioxide (one of the natural by-products of fermentation) can build up in your jars, so open your jar every few days to 'burp' your ferment – this will release the built-up carbon dioxide and prevent brine spilling out of the jar. Just be sure to press down your vegetables afterwards, so that the brine is still covering the top by at least 1 cm (½ inch).

Not only does fermenting extend the lives of vegetables, it also enhances their nutrient content and digestibility. Even better, consuming fermented foods introduces healthy probiotic bacteria into your gut, which may improve your overall health.

While lacto-fermentation is very safe, as with all food preparation, commonsense and good hygiene practices are needed. Cut away any bruised or perishing parts of your produce; keep your hands, benchtops and utensils scrupulously clean; and wash and sterilise your jars and lids (see page 181).

Once you've packed your produce into jars, fermentation should begin in a few days.

Don't be afraid to try your ferments to see how their flavour is developing. They require a little of your attention – but the reward is that they are foods that really love you back.

Here are some tips on what you need to keep an eye out for:

TIME

The longer you leave your ferment at room temperature, the more its flavour will develop, and the more probiotic bacteria it will contain. Open your jar after a couple of days and see what you think. Your ferment should smell pungent but not foul, and there may be some bubbles. Fermented vegetables have a sour, somewhat yeasty edge to them: think of sourdough bread, strong cheeses and beer.

Depending on the pace of the fermentation and how strong you want the flavour to be, you can leave your jar at room temperature (but out of direct sunlight) for anywhere from 2 days to 2 weeks before refrigerating. We suggest 2–7 days to start with, but (weather depending) you can ferment for up to 6 weeks.

Trust your palate and instinct when deciding whether your ferment is ready to be moved to the fridge. Your vegetables or fruit will continue to ferment in the fridge, but at a much slower rate, and will keep well for up to 6 months.

TEMPERATURE
In a hot climate, fermentation will be rapid, so during summer you'll probably need to transfer your ferments to the refrigerator after 2–3 days. Conversely, in cooler conditions, you may need to wait a week or two for fermentation to take place.

SPILLAGE
As fermentation occurs, you may find that the build-up of carbon dioxide forces liquid out of the jar. Just unscrew the lid of your jar and wipe down the rim and sides with paper towel or a clean damp cloth. If necessary, gently press the vegetables or fruit to resubmerge them in the liquid before replacing the lid.

SAFETY
Once fermentation is underway, the environment in the jar is hostile to harmful bacteria, so relax! Very rarely does anything go wrong. However, if any black mould develops on your ferment, throw the contents of that jar away. If a little white mould is visible on the surface, carefully scoop it off and check underneath: the rest of the ferment may well be fine.

Always trust your instincts, though, especially when you first start fermenting – if something doesn't smell or taste right, discard it.

PRACTICE MAKES PERFECT
When it comes to perfecting the art of fermenting foods, some trial and error is involved, so 'go with the flow', and with time and care you will be well rewarded.

Jaimee Edwards

Thank you

This book is a collection of preserving recipes from my home kitchen and from the Cornersmith Café, Picklery and Cooking School. The Cornersmith kitchens have always been filled with incredible cooks and makers who generously shared their creativity, their own food traditions and their love of preserving. A very big thank-you to all the Cornersmith picklers who filled jars with me over the last decade – so much love, so many laughs and so many delicious things to eat.

These recipes are for all the budding picklers out there. It is such an important food tradition; don't let it disappear. Make all the pickles, eat all the pickles and share your pickling skills.

Alex

Index

Published in 2025 by Murdoch Books, an imprint of Allen & Unwin

Murdoch Books Australia
Cammeraygal Country
83 Alexander Street
Crows Nest NSW 2065
Phone: +61 (0)2 8425 0100
murdochbooks.com.au
info@murdochbooks.com.au

Murdoch Books UK
Ormond House
26–27 Boswell Street
London WC1N 3JZ
Phone: +44 (0) 20 8785 5995
murdochbooks.co.uk
info@murdochbooks.co.uk

For corporate orders and custom publishing, contact our business development
team at salesenquiries@murdochbooks.com.au

Publishing director: Jane Morrow
Commissioning editor: Justin Wolfers
Editorial managers: Breanna Blundell and Julie Mazur Tribe
Design manager: Sharon Misko
Designer: Sharon Misko
Editor: Kay Halsey
Photographers: Alan Benson and Cath Muscat
Illustrator: AnneliesDraws
Stylists: David Morgan and Vanessa Austin
Production manager: Natalie Crouch

*Murdoch Books acknowledges the Traditional Owners of the Country on which we live and work.
We pay our respects to all Aboriginal and Torres Strait Islander Elders, past and present.*

A catalogue record for this
book is available from the
National Library of Australia

ISBN 978 1 76150 073 2

A catalogue record for this book is available from the British Library

Colour reproduction by Splitting Image Colour Studio Pty Ltd, Wantirna, Victoria

Printed by 1010 Printing International Limited, China

OVEN GUIDE: You may find cooking times vary depending on the oven you are using. For fan-forced ovens,
as a general rule, set the oven temperature to 20°C (25–50°F) lower than indicated in the recipe.

TABLESPOON MEASURES: We have used 20 ml (4 teaspoon) tablespoon measures. If you are using a
15 ml (3 teaspoon) tablespoon add an extra teaspoon of the ingredient for each tablespoon specified.

10 9 8 7 6 5 4 3 2 1